The
Fearful Flyers
Resource Guide

The
Fearful Flyers
Resource Guide

**Edited by Barry Elkus
with Murray E. Tieger, Ph.D.**

**Argonaut Entertainment, Inc.
Cincinnati, Ohio**

Argonaut Entertainment, Inc.
455 Delta Avenue, Suite 204
Cincinnati, Ohio 45226

ISBN #0-9637234-0-5
Library of Congress Catalog Card Number: 93-72363

Printed in the United States of America
First Edition

Acknowledgements

Over the past two years, a number of creative, energetic, and talented people have contributed to this project. Special thanks go to:

Leonard Dave, Harold Tieger, and Thomas Jackson, for their insight and feedback, from concept development through printing of the book.

Ann Lauer, for directing our exhaustive research efforts.

Perri Weinberg-Schenker, for her skillful writing and editing assistance.

Phyllis Jackson, for leading our enlightening consumer discussion groups.

Layne Flick, for lending her extensive travel industry expertise.

Jacqueline Mack at Magellan Travel, for sharing her insights during the formative stages of the book's development.

David Schansberg from Corporate Press Service, for providing his printing and technical advice and services.

Brad Rozen, for his research and production assistance.

Julie Nickell and Karen Henry, for their editing and proofing assistance and critical input on the book's promotion.

Sue Senefeld, for efficiently coordinating all production aspects of the book, including tracking and organizing mountains of information.

Julie Elkus, Sherri Tieger and Martha Dave, for their support, encouragement, and idea generation throughout this process.

Credits

Cover and Book Design:	Jim Kaelin and Julie Schauer at DesignMark, Inc.
Cartoon Illustrations By:	Roy Delgado, Woodbridge, Virginia
Printed By:	The C. J. Krehbiel Co., Cincinnati, Ohio

i

Table of Contents

Section 4

This section provides information on additional sources of help for the fearful flyer, including airports, travel agencies, travel organizations, state tourism boards and government agencies.

Section 5

This section offers a comprehensive guide to exciting travel options by car, motorcoach, boat or train, as well as adventure travel such as bicycling, hiking, rafting, and covered wagons.

Introduction

Argonaut Entertainment is a specialty publishing company in Cincinnati, Ohio. Our journey down this path started quite by accident a little more than two years ago, when we realized that one of our business partners was reluctant — in fact, afraid — to fly. Business trips had become a dreaded and draining experience for him. Vacation plans with his family were either put on hold or altered to feature weekend getaways by car.

At first, my reaction was typical of many people who learn that a friend or relative has a fear of flying. I joked about it a little bit and tried to reason with my partner that there was nothing to be afraid of. I reminded him of the conveniences of flying and the fun of escaping to the beach or other resort destinations. It became apparent that his fear was real, and that trying to minimize it was unproductive.

My intellectual curiosity took over at this point, and I began to do a little research on the fear of flying, also known as "aerophobia" or "aviaphobia." A local book store carried one book on the subject, which reported some very interesting statistics:

- during the last ten years, U.S. airlines have experienced an average annual fatality rate of 130 passengers;
- nearly 50,000 people die each year as a result of highway accidents;
- another 20,000 people die each year from accidents at home, including falling off ladders, down stairs and in bath tubs.

1

I proudly shared these data with my partner, who was unimpressed. Facts and figures alone were not the answer.

As I continued my research, I began to appreciate the scope of this problem: Between 25 and 50 million Americans have a fear of flying! Included among this group are some highly recognizable faces — Don Adams, Dana Carvey, Tony Curtis, Aretha Franklin, Wayne Gretzky, Florence Henderson, Stephen King, Evil Knievel, Stanley Kubrick, John Madden, Bob Newhart, Ronald Reagan, Gene Shallit, Carly Simon, and Chuck Yeager.

You'd think that with such a dramatic need, it would be easy to find resources and programs designed to help people overcome their fear. In fact, if you look hard enough, there are a number of very legitimate, professional, and effective resources that are accessible to people in all parts of the country. However, for the most part, these resources are a well-kept secret and have a low profile. My publishing instincts took over, and we decided to publish a resource guide to help people take the first step in overcoming their fear of flying.

We embarked upon a two year process to identify and understand the various types of resources available, from books and tapes to programs, seminars and clinics. Our exhaustive search included a review of newspaper and magazine articles on the subject; ordering and reading all of the books in print on the fear of flying; contacting airports in 75 major cities to identify local programs and resources; correspondence with all major airlines to understand their efforts in this area; consultation with several leaders in the travel agency industry; in-depth discussions with experts in psychiatry, psychology, and internal medicine; and networking with industry gurus who have spent good portions of their careers helping people overcome their fear of flying.

It's important to point out that this guide does not represent an endorsement of any particular book, program, or method of treatment. We have been careful not to evaluate or critique any of these resources; rather, we seek to present a complete profile based on our research and information provided by the specific author, program, clinic, or other source. It's also likely that we have not found every resource that is available. We encourage our readers to bring these undiscovered resources to our attention.

During the course of our research, we felt it essential to talk to fearful flyers about their fears and their efforts to overcome them. We ran a small ad in the local newspaper and received more than 300 responses that day from people who wanted to participate in our discussion groups. We ended up with four groups of ten, representing a variety of backgrounds, professions, and levels of fear. Some expressed discomfort and anxiety while flying; others reported panic attacks and a complete avoidance of air travel. Almost everyone reported some significant business or family disruption as a result of their fear. In fact, several responded to our ad based on the "suggestion" of their spouse.

When our discussion focused on steps that people had taken to overcome their fear, it became obvious that most participants were at a loss. A few had asked their physician to prescribe a mild sedative, and others admitted to indulging in more than one or two drinks during the flight. But most seemed resigned to live with their fear in spite of the consequences. When we began to describe some of the books, tapes, programs, and other resources that are available, they were both surprised and elated. They saw our resource guide as a convenient way to take control of the situation, and to do so at their own pace. Their interest and enthusiasm convinced us of the need to publish our resource guide.

We have organized this book into five sections, beginning with resources that you can use in the comfort and privacy of your own home. These include books and tapes developed by a variety of experts, from airline pilots to psychologists to former fearful flyers.

The second section is designed to help you decide if a clinical option is something you should consider. Dr. Murray E. Tieger, a clinical psychologist with more than 35 years of experience, describes the different types of providers who treat the fear of flying. He offers practical advice on how to identify a qualified practitioner in your community.

The third section offers a detailed profile of more than 35 fear of flying programs in cities across the country. These include airline programs, university programs, and programs offered by private clinics and organizations. Most involve some form of group interaction, and many culminate in an optional graduation flight. Almost all report "success rates" exceeding 80 percent.

The fourth section is a listing of other resources available in the community that offer help, either directly or indirectly, to the fearful flyer. These include airports, travel agencies, other travel organizations, state tourism bureaus, and a variety of government agencies.

The final section is our insurance policy: If all else fails, we've included a guide to exciting travel options you can enjoy without boarding an airplane. This section was compiled by Layne Flick, a travel professional with 18 years' experience in the industry and worldwide travel under her belt. Whether by boat, train, car, bus, or foot, Layne provides a variety of ways to see the country and the world while keeping your feet on the ground.

In case you're wondering about our business partner, he'll be receiving the first copy of our book as it rolls off the presses! We hope that this book helps him, as well as millions of others, take the first step toward overcoming their fear of flying.

Barry Elkus
President
Argonaut Entertainment, Inc.

1

AT YOUR PACE, AT YOUR PLACE: RESOURCES FOR USE AT HOME

1

At Your Pace, At Your Place: Resources For Use At Home

This section is designed to provide you with a comprehensive list of books and tape-based programs that have been developed specifically to help aerophobics address, understand, and overcome their fear of flying. These resources allow you to tackle your fear at your convenience and in the privacy of your home or office. You can find professional help — and you can do it at your own pace.

There is a wide array of information available; read through the profiles carefully before deciding which method—or methods— will be right for you.

Books

The following books, arranged alphabetically, have been written by a variety of experts in the field of aerophobia—some are experts by virtue of education, some are experts by virtue of having overcome their own fear of flying, and some are experts in the field of aviation. Each author has not only an individual style, but an individual approach to the problem of fearful flying. One may focus more on the mind/body connection, for example, and another may devote more time to aviation education. Therefore, to enable you to choose the book best suited to your personality and needs, we've equipped you with thorough summaries of each publication. We've also provided bibliographic information to make it easy for you to obtain the book you want.

Most of these publications are available through your local bookstore. If they're not on the shelf, you can probably place an order with the staff. Some may be in your public library, as well.

For those books available directly from the publisher, we've given the information necessary for ordering. Prices quoted are accurate as of this printing but are subject to change.

TITLE:

Avioanxiety Becomes Controlled: Now, Fly Without Fear

AUTHORS:

Jim Remington, Ph.D., and Leona Remington

PUBLISHER:

Inner Marker to Growth, St. Louis, 1992. 143 pages. Paperback.

ABOUT THE AUTHORS:

Jim and Leona Remington have coauthored numerous books on overcoming the fear of flying, including *I Am Cleared For Take-off* and *Avioanxiety Becomes Controlled: Riding on a Corporate Aircraft*. Dr. Remington is a private practice counselor with degrees in adult education, counseling psychology, and practical theology. An avid flyer, he began taking flying lessons at age 16 and now holds licenses for private and commercial aircraft. He also is rated as a flight instructor and has taught flying and ground school courses.

ABOUT THE BOOK:

The Remingtons write from a spiritual perspective. Their program calls for the reader to use affirmations, positive visualization, and other exercises in his or her attempt to overcome the fear of flying. The book includes a 24-page aviation glossary.

The first one-third of the book deals with introductory issues: a brief overview of Dr. Remington and his philosophy as it relates to flying; anonymous testimonials; technological advances on the horizon that will help with turbulence and wind shear; and the question of the fear of flying recurring during recovery.

The book moves into the nuts and bolts of airplane travel. The flight is separated into seven phases, with detailed explanations of each phase and suggestions for making each go smoothly. For instance, phase one, "Preparation at Home," includes tips on purchasing tickets, packing, and making advance visits to the airport.

Dr. Remington proceeds through the other six phases, touching on information such as the four physical laws involved in flight; the flight plan, back-up systems, and engines; descriptions of taxiing and take-off; weather conditions, including severe weather and lightning; descent and the impact of pressure changes to the ears; the changing sounds of the engines; and landing. Each phase ends with visualization exercises and affirmations.

COST:

$9.95

AVAILABILITY:

Check your local bookstore, call (314) 533-4150, or write:

> Dr. Jim and Leona Remington
> Inner Marker to Growth
> P. O. Box 23310
> St. Louis, MO 63156

TITLE:

Fearless Flying: The Complete Program for Relaxed Air Travel*

AUTHORS:

Albert G. Forgione, Ph.D., and Frederic M. Bauer

PUBLISHER:

Houghton Mifflin Co., Boston, 1980. 256 pages. Paperback.

ABOUT THE AUTHORS:

Albert Forgione treats phobics in his private practice, teaches psychology at Tufts University School of Dental Medicine, and is Director of the Institute for Psychology of Air Travel. He developed techniques known as Active Stress Coping, which are widely used in dentistry and which he teaches in a course for aerophobics at Boston's Logan Airport.

Frederic Bauer has written for both print and broadcast mediums. His training spans many fields, including psychology.

ABOUT THE BOOK:

The authors state in the introduction that this book integrates techniques from psychoanalysis, behavior therapy, psychophysiology, kinesiology (the mechanics of human movement), and nutrition. Information is supported by the use of anecdotes, illustrations, photographs, charts, graphs, checklists, and surveys.

The book first works toward an understanding of fear—its universality, when it's appropriate and inappropriate, and how it's fueled by fantasy. The authors introduce Active Stress Coping and look at

12

some internal stressors, including ear problems, TMJ syndrome, improper diet, and improper breathing.

The authors explain how they use four surveys and checklists to measure the reader's fear levels. They show the link between fear and nutrition, citing the impact of refined sugar, caffeine, tobacco, alcohol, and vitamins; and they look at hypoglycemic reactions and how the time of day affects nutritional needs.

Breathing and muscle relaxation exercises are part of the program, as is a chapter that advocates a positive attitude, thought-stopping techniques, and assertiveness training. Another step—which comes only after mastering relaxation and thought-stopping, is an involved program of systematic desensitization which gradually exposes the individual to fearful situations while he is in deep relaxation.

The authors also take the reader on a photographic tour through an airport and onto an airplane. They offer a short lesson in aero-dynamics and conclude with a detailed description of the reader's graduation flight. There is also an "Appendix for Professionals" included at the back of the book.

COST:

$10

AVAILABILITY:

Order by calling the Institute for Psychology of Air Travel at (617) 437-1811.

*See also *Fearless Flying: The Complete Program for Relaxed Air Travel* in the "Fear of Flying Programs" section, page 85.

TITLE:

Fearless Flying: A Passenger Guide to Modern Airline Travel

AUTHORS:

John Greist, M.D., and Georgia Greist, Ph.D.

PUBLISHER:

Nelson-Hall, Chicago, 1981. 124 pages. Hardcover.

ABOUT THE AUTHORS:

John Greist is trained in internal medicine and psychiatry and is Professor of Psychiatry at the University of Wisconsin-Madison. Georgia Greist is a translator of Hungarian fiction. The couple travel frequently and wrote this book to help themselves and others feel more informed, and thus more confident, about flying.

ABOUT THE BOOK:

This book is a synthesis of information derived from various sources, especially those that pertain to the field of aviation medicine. The Greists begin with a definition of flying phobia and place it in the context of larger fears, such as agoraphobia (fear of open spaces) and acrophobia (fear of heights). They attempt to dispel those fears by explaining how airplanes fly, including discussions on flapping wings, engine reliability, and air traffic control.

The book delves into the Greists' program of self-directed exposure therapy, which requires that the fearful flyer attack in increments those things that cause anxiety (visiting a travel agent, driving to the airport, etc.). The authors provide a sample diary of exposure treatment to illustrate how the program should work.

The focus turns to preflight considerations, such as medical needs; airplane food and the availability of special-diet menus; the impact of air travel on pregnancy; and air fares. The Greists concentrate on possible medical problems in flight, including airsickness and pain in the ear, sinus, and teeth; and they devote a chapter to the causes, symptoms, effects, and treatment of jet lag.

The authors also address safety issues, including cabin atmosphere, loss of cabin pressure, aircraft evacuation, and passenger behavior during emergencies. They discuss a number of "problem areas," ranging from traveling with children to skyjacking.

The book concludes with three appendices that may interest some passengers: "The Danger From Toxic Fumes," "Immunization Schedules," and "Anemia."

COST:
$21.95

AVAILABILITY:
Check your local bookstore, or call (312) 390-9446.

TITLE:

Fly Without Fear

AUTHORS:

Nate Cott and Stewart Kampel

PUBLISHER:

Henry Regnery Company, Chicago, 1973. 201 pages. Hardcover.

ABOUT THE AUTHORS:

Nate Cott once passed up a lucrative business opportunity because it would have required him to fly to Europe. He began a self-help group called Fly Without Fear, Inc. and now flies an average of once a month. Through his organization, he conducts courses and holds seminars and practice flights for fearful flyers— "Airfraidycats," he calls them.

Stewart Kampel is a writer for the *New York Times*.

ABOUT THE BOOK:

This book, like the organization for which it is named, culminates with the Airfraidycat taking a flight.

Fly Without Fear first offers arguments on why the reader *should* fly—the importance of vacations and the convenience of flight as a mode of travel. It reassures readers that they are not alone by giving examples of many Airfraidycats, including Jackie Gleason, Bob Newhart, Isaac Asimov, Carly Simon, and Ronald Reagan. The book examines the roots and workings of fear—including several specific phobias and, especially, the fear of death—and suggests how people can face their fears.

On the premise that well-informed is well-assured, the book delves into a study of the aviation industry, including safety records, pilot and crew training, flight technology, and skyjacking. It teaches ways to conquer fear, such as relaxation exercises, yoga, meditation, and biofeedback.

The book concludes with information to make the trip go smoothly—advice on everything from traveling during peak hours and seasons, reservations, and special meals, to motion sickness, packing, flight insurance, and seat selection.

AVAILABILITY:

This book is out of print, but it's still available at many public libraries.

TITLE:

Fly Without Fear*

AUTHORS:

Carol L. Stauffer, M.S.W., and Captain Frank Petee

PUBLISHER:

Fly Without Fear, Pittsburgh, 1988. 164 pages. Paperback.

ABOUT THE AUTHORS:

Carol Stauffer is a therapist specializing in behavior modification methods. Frank Petee is an airline professional with more than 45 years of experience in commercial aviation. Together, they direct USAir's Fearful Flyers Program.

ABOUT THE BOOK:

Fly Without Fear is based on USAir's program, which was developed in 1975 and has served more than 5,000 people. The program employs a combined approach of behavior modification (relaxation training, thought-stopping, and desensitization) and aviation education (information about pilot training, airplane operation, and weather conditions). The authors use case studies and "thoughts to fly by"—reassuring bits of information about flying—and provide a ten-page photo section to acquaint fearful flyers with the airport and airplane.

The book begins with a discussion of fear in general and fear of flying in particular. It highlights the misconceptions that can add to people's fears—for example, the belief that a silent engine is a dead engine—and gives factual responses in an attempt to ease those fears. The authors continue with a study of turbulence and other weather conditions, such as lightning, fog, and wind shear.

The next several chapters alternate between behavior modification training and airplane safety and maintenance. The authors include information on bodily responses to fear and provide a four-week desensitization plan; and they look at quality assurance and the roles of airline professionals, including mechanics, flight attendants, dispatchers, air traffic controllers, and the FAA.

Finally, the authors focus on the readiness of both the reader and the aircraft. They guide the passenger through all the phases, from planning a trip, to getting to the airport, to boarding the plane, to the actual flight. Similarly, they go through a checklist for the airplane: the crew's preparation, fuel needs, a walkaround inspection, the flight plan, air traffic control clearance, takeoff, flight, and landing.

COST:
$9.95

AVAILABILITY:
Check your local bookstore, or order by sending $9.95 plus $2.00 shipping and handling to:

    Carol L. Stauffer and Frank Petee
    P. O. Box 15410
    Pittsburgh, PA 15237

*See also USAir Fearful Flyers Program in the "Fear of Flying Programs" section, page 76.

TITLE:

Flying Can Be Fun: A Guide for the White-Knuckled Flyer

AUTHOR:

Edie Grande

PUBLISHER:

Dyenamiks, Inc., Middleton, MA, 1990. 71 pages. Paperback.

ABOUT THE AUTHOR:

Edie Grande is an ex-phobic who now enjoys flying.

ABOUT THE BOOK:

Flying Can Be Fun takes its cues from its title. It approaches the subject of fearful flying in a positive, humorous manner. Written not for the phobic who avoids flying at all costs but for the "uncomfortable flyer," *Flying Can Be Fun* tackles the discomfort by merging cartoon illustration, factual snippets, tips, and informational copy.

The book begins with an overview of air safety and the stringent standards for maintenance and crew training. It goes into the aerodynamics of flying, giving basic information about the engines, wings, and rudder; what happens before and during takeoff; and what sounds to expect during landing. It also argues against some common myths, such as the high risk of midair collision and the dangers of turbulence and lightning.

The author discusses the physical discomforts of flying, from motion sickness and ear pain to dry skin, back pain, and excessive heat or cold. She proceeds to the topic of anxiety, including an anxiety-reducing diet, relaxation exercises, thought-stopping techniques, imagery, and drugs and alcohol.

A section of tips for hassle-free flying includes advice on special meals, promotional fares, trip cancellation insurance, and getting bumped. It also provides medical tips, especially for foreign travel; and it gives information about travel documents, airport security, and avoiding airport hassles.

Then the author offers advice for flying with children, with pets, or with white-knuckled flyers; or with someone who is pregnant, handicapped, or elderly. She concludes with a list of therapists and phobia clinics that specialize in the fear of flying.

COST:
$6.95

AVAILABILITY:
Check your local bookstore.

TITLE:

How to Master Your Fear of Flying

AUTHOR:

Albert Ellis, Ph.D.

PUBLISHER:

Institute for Rational Living, New York, 1972. 136 pages. Paperback.

ABOUT THE AUTHOR:

Albert Ellis holds a Ph.D. in clinical psychology and has extensive experience in both academic and clinical settings. His other books include *A Guide to Rational Living* and *Sex Without Guilt.* Dr. Ellis conquered his own fear of flying before writing this book.

ABOUT THE BOOK:

Dr. Ellis first explains how he used a therapeutic approach called "rational-emotive psychotherapy" to overcome his fear of flying. He expands that fear to encompass the fear of death and makes 12 arguments why worrying about death is counterproductive.

He proceeds to look at the underlying reasons for unnecessary anxiety. He explains how people perpetuate negative beliefs by repeating them to themselves and demonstrates how to question those beliefs.

Dr. Ellis shows how people use anxiety as a defense mechanism. He begins to assign flying "homework"— that is, having the reader commit to taking a certain number of flights within a certain time period—and emphasizes the importance of setting and meeting deadlines. He incorporates into the program various other methods, such as desensitization, reinforcement, and relaxation.

Dr. Ellis follows this with a somewhat scholarly discussion of other methods of combating anxiety. These include positive suggestion, rational-emotive imagery, religion, self-hypnosis, self-analysis, and the use of drugs. He acknowledges the possibility of an actual emergency, such as a hijacking, and demonstrates the futility of worrying about it. He concludes with an affirmation of the joy of living an anxiety-free existence.

COST:

$4.95

AVAILABILITY:

Check your local bookstore, or call (212) 353-0822.

TITLE:
The Joy of Flying: Overcoming the Fear*

AUTHOR:
W. H. Gunn, Ph.D.

PUBLISHER:
Wings Publications, Mission, Kansas, 1987. 118 pages. Hardcover.

ABOUT THE AUTHOR:
Walter Gunn is both a pilot and a psychologist. He flew for TWA for 39 years, logging more than 28,000 flying hours and 1,000 ocean crossings. He now teaches college courses in both psychiatry and aviation.

ABOUT THE BOOK:
The Joy of Flying is written for the true aerophobic, whom Dr. Gunn describes as someone who expends great effort to avoid flying. The book makes liberal use of anecdotes to highlight its points.

To explain aerophobia, Dr. Gunn defines contributing elements such as fear, anxiety, and stress. He looks at various treatments, including behavior modification and assertiveness training, and explains why he advocates a mix of approaches.

Dr. Gunn examines the "mind-body connection" by describing anatomy and body chemistry as they relate to fear, and he looks at the fight-or-flight phenomenon. He offers a personality profile of aerophobics, characterized by four behavior patterns: generalized anxiety, problems of personal control, claustrophobia, and separation anxiety. He follows with eight case studies.

The book also looks at ways to gain control over fear. It addresses breathing, cognitive thought conditioning, biofeedback, stress innoculation, and medication. Finally, the book provides information about air safety, technology, weather, and air traffic, as well as the airline industry's commitment to pilot and crew training.

COST:

$16.95

AVAILABILITY:

Check your local bookstore, or order by writing:

Wings Publications

P. O. Box 161

Mission, KS 66201

Books ordered directly from the publisher can be autographed on request.

*See also The Joy of Flying: Overcoming the Fear in the "Fear of Flying Programs" section, page 119.

TITLE:

Just In Case: A Passenger's Guide to Airplane Safety and Survival

AUTHOR:

Daniel A. Johnson, Ph.D.

PUBLISHER:

Plenum Press, New York and London, 1984. 261 pages. Hardcover.

ABOUT THE AUTHOR:

Daniel Johnson is an expert in the field of airplane safety and a psychologist who treats passengers and crew members involved in aircraft accidents. A former head of McDonnell-Douglas Corporation's Passenger Safety Program, Dr. Johnson now serves as president of Interaction Research Corporation, a company that specializes in airline crew training and passenger safety information.

ABOUT THE BOOK:

Dr. Johnson's approach is to educate the reader on pragmatic issues related to airplane safety. Rather than treat the fear of flying, *Just In Case* addresses that which passengers fear most—an aircraft emergency—and teaches the reader how best to handle such an emergency. The book makes extensive use of case studies, examples, and statistics to illustrate its points.

Just In Case begins with a look at the relative safety of aircraft travel and defines the various types of possible accidents. Dr. Johnson gives a thorough explanation of how people react to emergencies, including the panic response and what he terms "behavioral inaction," or freezing.

There is an examination of each particular type of emergency: Dr. Johnson outlines what to expect, describes the emergency equipment that may be available, and gives guidelines on how passengers should behave. He talks about what may be the myth of pinpointing "safe" seat locations. There is a detailed explanation of emergency exits and survival techniques, supported by diagrams, charts, and step-by-step illustrations to further clarify instructions.

The author also discusses post-accident stress, including psychological and psychosomatic stress reactions, survivor guilt, and fear of flying. He concludes with guidelines for accident survivors and instructions on when and how to select professional help.

COST:
$19.95

AVAILABILITY:
Check your local bookstore, or order by calling (800) 221-9369.

TITLE:

Learning to Fly Without Fear: The Easy, Step-By-Step Guide to Anxiety-Free Flying

AUTHOR:

Ken Hutchins

PUBLISHER:

Berkley Books, New York, 1990. 133 pages. Paperback.

ABOUT THE AUTHOR:

Ken Hutchins is a pilot, a former manager of training for a major airline, and a licensed psychotherapist.

ABOUT THE BOOK:

Learning to Fly Without Fear begins with a basic lesson in airline history, emphasizing the safety of airplane travel and the thorough training of the crews. It provides preflight planning advice: how to obtain the lowest fare; the difference between first class and coach; special services; and seating. It also offers some tips for first-time flyers and describes the actual flight, including turbulence and night flying.

The book goes on to define fear and phobia. The author identifies various phobias, discusses getting control of fear, and includes a questionnaire to help you understand the basis of your anxiety. He examines the physical symptoms of fear, including shortness of breath, hyperventilation, muscle tension, heart palpitations, dizziness, vomiting, and fainting.

Mr. Hutchins outlines a plan for fear recovery; he gives examples but also stresses that the reader should customize his or her own plan. He addresses the importance of confronting fears, of communicating, and of being tenacious. He also gives specifics on reducing panic; positive self-talk; patience and acceptance; and changing attitudes. Lessons in active relaxation follow, and the book concludes with a preflight checklist.

COST:

$4.95

AVAILABILITY:

Check your local bookstore.

TITLE:

White Knuckles: Getting Over the Fear of Flying

AUTHOR:

Layne Ridley

PUBLISHER:

Doubleday & Company, Inc., Garden City, New York, 1987. 139 pages. Paperback.

ABOUT THE AUTHOR:

Layne Ridley is a writer and former fearful flyer. She interviewed experts, studied statistics, and conducted other research to overcome her own fear before writing this book.

ABOUT THE BOOK:

White Knuckles is a compilation of information obtained from thorough research—the acknowledgements list dozens of experts the author interviewed. Ms. Ridley writes from a first-person perspective and interjects witty remarks and anecdotes throughout the book.

She begins with a chapter called "The Perfectly Sensible Fear of Flying," which details why so many people share this fear and what the basis of it might be. She offers a detailed description of typically fearful thoughts, followed by factual explanations rooted in airplane design and the principles of flight.

The author deals with passengers' reluctance to put their lives in others' hands. She explains why the "others' hands" are capable hands, giving details of developmental and certification testing, maintenance, FAA regulations, and air traffic control. She offers some insight into airplane accidents: that they are rare but *do* exist, how professionals handle them, and how to survive them.

The focus of the book turns to guiding the reader through a flight. This section includes relaxation and thought-stopping techniques, visits to the airport, and other coping mechanisms. The author ends with a description of her own progress, followed by miscellaneous information in four appendices: a sample hierarchy of fearful situations; a relaxation routine; a summary of fatal U. S. airline accidents; and organizations, agencies, and other resources.

COST:
$6.95

AVAILABILITY:
Check your local bookstore.

There are literally scores of books on the market aimed at relieving fears, phobias, anxiety, and panic attacks. While they don't focus exclusively on the fear of flying, the following books offer insights and suggestions that can be put to use in your efforts to overcome aerophobia.

TITLE:
Beyond Fear

AUTHORS:
Robert Handly with Pauline Neff

PUBLISHER:
Fawcett Crest, New York, 1987. 261 pages. Paperback.

ABOUT THE BOOK:
Features of this book include a five-step program called FEAR-Smashers; a 14-day plan to start alleviating fear; instructions to the phobic's "support person"; and advice to people with specific fears, including the fear of flying. The book also addresses the various options for treating fear, the mind-body connection, and relaxation techniques.

COST:
$4.95

AVAILABILITY:
Check your local bookstore.

TITLE:

Don't Panic: Taking Control of Anxiety Attacks

AUTHOR:

R. Reid Wilson, Ph.D.

PUBLISHER:

Harper & Row, New York, 1986. 262 pages. Paperback.

ABOUT THE BOOK:

Don't Panic is arranged in two parts. Part one focuses on identifying the problem of panic, and part two teaches ways to take control of anxiety attacks. Much of the second part is devoted to understanding the inner voice, or "observer," and retraining it to play a positive, supportive role, rather than a negative, hopeless, or critical role. There are also lessons in visualization, breathing, and relaxation.

COST:

$11

AVAILABILITY:

Check your local bookstore.

TITLE:

**The Good News About Panic, Anxiety, and Phobias:
Cures, Treatments, and Solutions in the New Age
of Biopsychiatry**

AUTHOR:

Mark S. Gold, M.D.

PUBLISHER:

Bantam Books, New York, 1989. 297 pages. Paperback.

ABOUT THE BOOK:

This book, written by a biopsychiatrist, focuses on
the interrelationship between behavior and the brain. It
explores the biological basis of panic and describes
medical problems that can mask themselves as panic. It
presents treatment options, most of which involve
medications but which also include behavior therapy,
exercise, additional exposure to sun, and more.

COST:

$12.95

AVAILABILITY:

Check your local bookstore.

TITLE:

Overcoming Panic Attacks: Strategies to Free Yourself from the Anxiety Trap*

AUTHORS:

Shirley Babior, L.C.S.W., M.F.C.C., and Carol Goldman, L.I.C.S.W. Shirley Babior has treated aerophobics in her practice for 17 years.

PUBLISHER:

CompCare Publishers, Minneapolis, 1990. 96 pages. Paperback.

ABOUT THE BOOK:

Overcoming Panic Attacks explores physiological, cognitive, and behavioral methods of reducing anxiety, such as deep breathing and thought-focusing. It provides exercises to help the reader evaluate feelings, fears, and progress. One section addresses relapses, and another provides guidance to friends and relatives who want to help. The book concludes with ten personal accounts from individuals who have broken their cycle of panic and withdrawal.

COST:

$6.95 plus shipping. The publisher offers a discount schedule for orders of multiple copies.

AVAILABILITY:

To order, call (800) 328-3300 or fax to (612) 559-2415.

*See also Center for Anxiety and Stress Treatment in the "Fear of Flying Programs" section, page 127.

Additionally, a comprehensive understanding of aviation and flight principles can be a powerful tool in fighting aerophobia. For those interested in expanding their knowledge about flight operations, the following book can be helpful.

TITLE:
Understanding Flying

AUTHOR:
Richard L. Taylor

PUBLISHER:
Thomasson-Grant, Charlottesville, Virginia, 1977. 329 pages. Hardcover.

ABOUT THE BOOK:
This book was written for an audience of pilots but uses language that's easily understood. Its structure is in four parts. Part one is devoted to the airplane and how it flies; part two deals with takeoffs, landings, weather, flight instruments, and aerial navigation; part three is about airspace, rules of the air, and airports; and part four focuses on human elements, including pilot certification, psychological factors, and emergencies.

COST:
$29.95

AVAILABILITY:
Check your local bookstore, or call (800) 999-1780.

Tape-Based Programs

In addition to books, a number of other resources have been developed for individualized use. All of these programs make use of audiotapes, with additional components including everything from instructional booklets to "flight fragrances." These resources have all been developed by experts in the field of aerophobia.

PROGRAM:

Fearless Flying: The Complete Program for Relaxed Air Travel

DEVELOPED BY:

Albert G. Forgione, Ph.D. Dr. Forgione is Director of the Institute for Psychology of Air Travel, which sponsors seminars for aerophobics as well as this home-study course. Dr. Forgione has specialized in aerophobia since 1972.

COMPONENTS:

The book *Fearless Flying: The Complete Program for Relaxed Air Travel*, four audiotapes, and an instructional booklet.

COST:

$59.95, post-paid. You can also buy the book separately for $10, and each individual tape is available for $15.

TO ORDER:

Contact the Institute at (617) 437-1811, or write:
    Institute for Psychology of Air Travel
    Suite 300
    25 Huntington Ave.
    Boston, MA 02116

ABOUT THE PROGRAM:

The book, tapes, and booklet are designed to present a structured program, with each component functioning hand-in-hand with the others. The instructional booklet leads you through each sequence, informing you when to read which chapter, when to listen to which tape, and when to practice which skills.

The tapes, each of which lasts 90 minutes, deal with the following:

• Tape 1, side 1, "Fearless Flying." This provides a relaxation exercise, recorded in a male voice with cued in flight sounds, and a general discussion of anxiety and fear.

• Tape 1, side 2, "Coping With Stress of Air Travel." An overview of the nature of air travel fear and coping techniques.

• Tape 2, "Active Stress Coping." This teaches the technique Dr. Forgione developed for use in dentistry, which he also applies to the treatment of aerophobics. The tape reiterates the relaxation exercise from the first tape, followed by a discussion of antistress lifestyle.

• Tape 3, "A Flight Captain Answers Questions." Captain Gould "Mac" McIntyre, a retired Pan American pilot with 30 years of flying experience in Boeing 707s and 747s, answers a wide range of typical questions posed by aerophobics.

• Tape 4, side 1, "Guided Flight to Portland." This provides an individually guided relaxation exercise, taped on an actual flight to Portland, Oregon.

• Tape 4, side 2, "Comments of Former Phobics" and "Relaxation Exercise." On this tape, you'll hear former aerophobics talk about their fears and successes. The tape also repeats the relaxation exercise, this time recorded in a female voice.

The program requires that you devote at least ten weeks to it. It encompasses regularly practicing the breathing and relaxation exercises, following an antistress diet, working on thought-stopping and other cognitive changes, and incrementally desensitizing yourself to airport and airplane experiences.

PROGRAM:
Help for the Fearful Flyer

DEVELOPED BY:

Captain T. W. Cummings, who originated "The Program for the Fearful Flyer" for Pan American Airways in 1975. Since then, he has led seminars for fearful flyers in most U.S. cities and in London.

COMPONENTS:

Two audiotapes and an accompanying booklet.

COST:

$28

TO ORDER:

Send a check, payable to Freedom From Fear of Flying, Inc., to:

Freedom From Fear of Flying, Inc.
2021 Country Club Prado
Coral Gables, FL 33134
For more information, call (305) 621-7042.

ABOUT THE PROGRAM:

This self-help home study course is a prerequisite for Captain Cummings' seminar program, but it's also designed to help the aerophobic who can't attend a seminar.

The first tape serves as an introduction to the course. One side teaches the program's relaxation method, and the other teaches ways to let go of your fear. The second tape details the airport and the flight experience. It discusses the procedures, sounds, and movements that take place on the jet airplane, from boarding to disembarking.

The booklet, *Answers to 75 Questions About Flight and About Fear,* provides answers to questions about safety, flight, and fear. Captain Cummings selected the questions from those most frequently posed to him by fearful flyers. He also includes an article by Robert J. Serling, "Safety Is First"; a section of tips for the anxious flyer; and some encouraging quotations.

PROGRAM:

Pathway Systems' "Achieving Comfortable Flight" series

DEVELOPED BY:

R. Reid Wilson, Ph.D., and Captain T.W. Cummings. Dr. Wilson is the author of *Don't Panic: Taking Control of Anxiety Attacks, Stop Obsessing! How to Overcome Your Obsessions and Compulsions,* and *Breaking the Panic Cycle: Self-Help for People With Phobias.* Captain Cummings is Director of "The Program for the Fearful Flyer," a seminar series he developed in 1975 for Pan American Airways.

COMPONENTS:

Two booklets, four audiotapes, one set of quick reference cards.

COST:

$59.95 plus $2.50 shipping. The company offers a money-back guarantee.

TO ORDER:

Call (800) 394-2299.

ABOUT THE PROGRAM:

Pathway Systems produces a range of guidance programs for personal development. The "Achieving Comfortable Flight" series includes the following:

• *Personal Strategies* booklet, by R. Reid Wilson (68 pages). A step-by-step guide to increase comfort and enjoyment during flight. The booklet focuses on these issues: managing worries before and during flight; responding to uncomfortable physical symptoms; muscle relaxation skills; breathing skills; thought-stopping exercises; overcoming the fear of heights and closed-in spaces; and fears during takeoff, turbulence, and other weather conditions.

• *The Flight Experience* booklet, by Captain T. W. Cummings (60 pages). A detailed discussion of the commercial flight experience. Features of this booklet include: a flight description encompassing 75 sights, sounds, and sensations encountered on a routine flight; encouraging facts about weather; an explanation of turbulence; facts about the air traffic control system and flight safety; maintenance and aerodynamics of aircraft; and the health requirements, qualifications, and ongoing training of flight crews.

• Quick Reference Cards. A set of 14 cards summarizing the primary self-help strategies to use prior to and during a flight. Designed to be easily accessible, these are small enough to carry in a purse or briefcase.

• Tape 1, "Introduction" (22 minutes). This provides an overview of what it takes to fly comfortably and introduces you to the most effective way to use this series.

• Tape 2, "Practicing Your Breathing Skills" (18 minutes). This teaches three straightforward and simple breathing skills to relieve stress.

• Tape 3, side 1, "Associating With the Positive" (14 minutes). This is the first of three sessions that use guided imagery. During this exercise, you learn to associate positive feelings while achieving comfortable flight.

• Tape 3, side 2, "Creating Comfort From Distress" (17 minutes). The guided imagery on this tape teaches

43

how to reduce tension and return to a calm state within minutes.

• Tape 4, side 1, "Rehearsing Your Coping Skills" (16 minutes). During this guided imagery, you "see" yourself in five flight scenes that typically cause stress. You try various skills and determine which are helpful. This tape also helps condition you to respond to your symptoms before and during flight.

• Tape 4, side 2, "Generalized Relaxation and Imagery" (18 minutes). These are suggestions and images to help you let go of your tensions. The tape is designed to be used any time you want to relax, including during a flight.

PROGRAM:

SOAR Inc. Seminars on Aeroanxiety Relief

DEVELOPED BY:

Captain Tom Bunn, a commercial airline captain and licensed therapist.

COMPONENTS:

The program is in three parts—psychology, aviation, and practical applications—each containing audiotapes, a manual, and a question-and-answer sheet. SOAR can be combined with AART (aeroanxiety relief therapy), which is two one-hour sessions conducted in person or by phone with either Captain Bunn or Elaine Rapp, a therapist who works closely with Captain Bunn.

COST:

SOAR alone costs $285, which can be paid in full or in three- or five-month installments. SOAR plus AART costs $390, also available in installments. You can borrow the first set of materials free for a trial run. The company offers a money-back guarantee.

TO ORDER:

Call (800) FEAR FLY (332-7359), or write:

SOAR Inc.
P. O. Box 747
Westport, CT 06881

Payment can be made by credit card or check.

ABOUT THE PROGRAM:

SOAR began in 1975 as a seminar conducted by Captain Bunn. The tape-based program was developed as a substitute for people who could not attend the seminars. It soon became clear, however, that clients achieved better results with the tapes than the seminars. The program is now available only in the tape version, with or without the two-session therapy.

The first section of SOAR focuses on the psychology of aerophobia. Section two is a complete study of aviation. Section three teaches a step-by-step approach to apply what you've learned in the first two sections.

Clients have flown after going through the program in a week's time, but Captain Bunn recommends spending about five minutes per day for six weeks on the program. The company's toll-free number is available any time you have a question or just want to discuss the material.

The optional AART was developed to provide individualized support and to augment the SOAR program. It combines elements from six disciplines: Gestalt therapy, cognitive therapy, expressive therapy, Alexander technique, NLP neurolinguistics, and bioenergetic therapy.

SOAR has been featured in *Newsweek,* the *New York Times*, the *Boston Globe,* and on "Good Morning America."

PROGRAM:

TERRAP Programs

DEVELOPED BY:

Arthur B. Hardy, M.D. Dr. Hardy is the father of "contextual therapy" and the founder of TERRAP Anxiety and Phobia Treatment Center at White Plains Hospital Center in White Plains, New York.

COMPONENTS:

TERRAP offers a variety of at-home options for aerophobics. The flying video package includes one videotape, one audiotape, and an accompanying workbook. There are two separate audiotapes that deal specifically with aerophobia: "Flying Safety" and "Desensitization to Airplanes." The system also has numerous other products for use at home that deal with phobias in general.

COST:

$45.99 for the video package. The audiotapes are $11 each.

TO ORDER:

Contact TERRAP at (800) 2-PHOBIA or (415) 327-1312, or write:

TERRAP
932 Evelyn Street
Menlo Park, CA 94025

ABOUT THE PROGRAM:

The videotape takes you through a step-by-step process that includes learning about fear reduction techniques; the impact of attitude and knowledge on recovery; and avoiding extraneous stress factors while working on desensitization. The accompanying audiotape is designed for use on the plane.

"Flying Safety" is an audiotape that consists of a question-and-answer session with a pilot. "Desensitization to Airplanes" is a preflight relaxation and desensitization exercise led by Dr. Hardy.

PROGRAM:

THAIRAPY Flight Relaxation Training

DEVELOPED BY:

Glen Arnold, Ph.D., an aviation psychologist, commercial pilot, and Director of THAIRAPY. Dr. Arnold has been involved in counseling for more than 20 years and has been a pilot for more than 30 years, having first soloed at the age of 18. He writes a monthly column, "Aviation Psychology," for the *Pacific Flyer Aviation News*.

COMPONENTS:

The Audio Cassette Flight Kit includes a two-sided relaxation tape, an air travel book, a wrist band, a visualization button, and instructions for use. Also available are "flight fragrances," with six aromas to choose from.

COST:

The tape kit costs $21.95, plus $3 shipping. Flight fragrance oils come in .25 fluid ounce bottles and are $9.95 each, plus $2 shipping.

TO ORDER:

Call (714) 756-1133 and ask for order forms, or write:
THAIRAPY
4500 Campus Drive
Suite 628F
Newport Beach, CA 92660-1814

ABOUT THE PROGRAM:

THAIRAPY began in 1978 and exists today as a full-service training program, offering seminars, individual counseling, and at-home options for aerophobics. The

49

Audio Cassette Flight Kit is designed for practice before the flight and for use during it. It focuses on teaching deep muscle relaxation and comes with a two-week, money-back guarantee.

The flight fragrances were developed based on research that demonstrates a link between scents and mood. They are designed to be an aid to managing symptoms of discomfort. There is a scent to correspond to each of these conditions: preflight anxiety, confinement/claustrophobia, feelings of panic, labored breathing, flight-related insomnia, and the desire to increase relaxation.

2

FINDING PROFESSIONAL HELP

"Don't worry…it's just something
going around."

2

Finding Professional Help

By Murray E. Tieger, Ph.D.

"I traveled here by train because I'm *terrified* of flying."

"When I have to go to the West Coast on business, I drive. It takes forever, but I'm too afraid to fly."

For anyone who has a fear of flying, or *aerophobia*, these statements must strike a chord. The anticipation—of a fatal crash, of suffocating, of losing control—is so powerful that it tends to preclude any change in behavior. Even at the cost of serious interference with your work or social functioning, the fear of being exposed, of embarrassing or humiliating yourself, results in avoidance. Given the expectation of catastrophe, your thought process is, "If I avoid the dangerous situation, I can escape the pain and catastrophe." The intense, disabling, and often overwhelming fear overrides the consequences to your work or social life.

The word *phobia* comes from the Greek *phobos*, meaning terror and flight. One of the most common yet crippling phobias is *agoraphobia*, which is literally the fear of being in open spaces. Closely allied are the so-called "simple phobias" involving a more limited fear, such as that of heights, the dark, cats — or flying. The fear of flying, like other simple phobias, involves a fear that intensifies as you approach the frightening situation. Often, this fear accelerates despite your knowledge that the anxiety is out of proportion to the actual danger. Faced with the feared situation, you become almost immediately anxious: Your heart beat becomes rapid, you perspire, you feel nauseous, and you avoid the feared object or situation.

Such phobic responses are relatively common. Typically, the person experiencing the phobia at best will be able to endure the situation only with intense anxiety, bordering on panic. It may matter little to know that your phobia is a fear displaced from an unconscious conflict to a conscious object. It may matter little that your fear is unreasonable. It may matter even less that your livelihood is in jeopardy. What *may* make a difference, however, is knowing that there are now a number of routes you may take to help you modify and even overcome your fear. Sections One and Three of this book describe self-help and specific fear of flying program options; this section focuses on the medical and clinical options available to you through individual and group therapy.

The benefits of living a fuller, more comfortable life, with increased self-esteem and sense of control, far outweigh any stigma you may feel about being helped.

Seeking Professional Help

Ordinarily, your degree of discomfort is the most accurate barometer of a decision to seek professional help. Clearly, disabling anxiety or apprehensiveness is difficult to live with and would be a compelling reason to seek help. With aerophobia, the anxiety is minimized by the act of avoidance: You feel better when you know you do not have to fly. Even here, though, a vague, persistent apprehension lurks in the background, interfering with your sense of adequacy and self-esteem and casting a pall on future planning. Family vacations, pleasure trips, and other nonessential travel are shelved.

An equally urgent reason to seek professional help centers on interference with your job performance. Working on the 48th floor of a building and developing an elevator phobia clearly are incompatible. Similarly, if your job requires even sporadic travel to distant sites, the prospect of flying would pose insurmountable conflict. With your livelihood at stake, consulting a physician or therapist becomes a necessity.

Family Physicians

Family physicians, by virtue of their training, can be an excellent starting point. They can help you choose the most appropriate treatment, and they can also prescribe a broad array of mild tranquilizing or antidepressant medications that will temper the acute discomfort and allow you to begin to expose yourself in small doses to the process of flying.

Family physicians also can listen to the history of your fear and make suggestions that will be helpful.

When more specialized intervention is indicated, they can make the most appropriate referral, to a psychologist, psychiatrist, social worker, or other licensed clinical counselor. If your doctor is unaware of resources in your community, you can contact the Department of Psychology at a local university, the Department of Psychiatry at a medical school, or a local mental health organization.

Psychiatrists

Psychiatrists have a medical degree and should have completed a three- or four-year residency in psychiatry. After two years of postresidency practice, they may take an oral and written examination, under the auspices of the American Board of Psychiatry and Neurology, and become board-certified. Their training should equip them to administer psychotherapy and antianxiety and antidepressant medication, but you still will need to ascertain their training in behavior modification techniques, which are described in detail later in this section.

Psychologists

Licensed psychologists usually have doctoral degrees (Ph.D., Psy.D., or Ed.D.). They have specialized clinical training and have graduated from programs approved by the American Psychological Association. They may be listed in the *National Register of Health Service Providers*, available in your local library. They may also be credentialed by the American Board of Professional Psychology, which means they have passed an examination and have had their experiences reviewed by the board. As licensing and certification procedures vary from state to state, you should check psychologists' credentials and ascertain their familiarity and experience with various treatment vehicles, especially behavior modification techniques.

Psychiatric Social Workers

Psychiatric social workers must have at least two years of graduate training in a program accredited by the Council on Social Work Education. In addition, to be certified by the Academy of Certified Social Workers, they must have a master's or doctoral degree in social work, at least two years of postdegree experience, membership in the National Association of Social Workers, and have passed a written examination. Social workers generally are most experienced in psychotherapy aimed at resolving tensions in interpersonal relationships and tensions brought about by personal conflicts.

Treatment Options

Your selection of a practitioner, at least in part, will be determined by the method of treatment indicated. Some methods, such as relaxation techniques, are used by several classes of therapists; others, such as the use of medication, are the domain of only one or two types of practitioner. Below is a look at those options to consider in the treatment of aerophobia.

Behavior Modification Techniques

Several methods of treatment fall under the category of "behavior modification techniques." These techniques tend to be widely used in treating aerophobia. They are aimed at changing your behavior without exploring past experience or internal conflict.

Systematic desensitization. Also known as *in-vivo* (meaning, literally, "in the living body") exposure, this behavior modification approach is the most widely used and perhaps most effective of the treatment options. Based on principles of learning and conditioning, it involves graduated exposure to the phobic situation, along a hierarchy of anxieties that you and the therapist have established together. Exposure may begin with visual imagery or a detailed description of the airport, airplane, or flight experience; gradually it advances to establishing gentle contact with the process of trip-planning, flying, and the airplane itself. Behavioral change is reinforced by the therapist's positive approval and by the sense of relief associated with the diminished anxiety. The final objective of anxiety-free flight is accompanied by improved self-esteem and a restored sense of self-control.

Cognitive restructuring. The therapist using this method would teach you to reevaluate your thoughts and beliefs about flying. This technique challenges your negative, dysfunctional thinking and, in a very neutral setting, allows you to confront those beliefs, correct misconceptions, and try more behavioral change. This method is especially effective in increasing self-confidence when it is combined with training in social skills, such as sharing feelings, being assertive, and taking initiative with others near you. Talking with the flight crew also can be rewarding and reinforcing.

Relaxation training. Relaxation training often is used in the context of psychotherapy and in conjunction with other behavior modification techniques. You would be taught to breathe deeply and slowly, to attend to the mechanics of your breathing, and in the process to relax the neuromuscular underpinnings of your intense apprehension. Deep-muscle relaxation also can be taught in a relatively brief time, enabling you to be fully relaxed before a flight.

Hypnosis and biofeedback. The above relaxation techniques can be extended readily, if necessary, into hypnosis and self-hypnosis. Rescued from the era of stage demonstration, hypnosis is now a well-respected, reputable technique. It is an easily taught total relaxation method, in which you retain full control over your status and are able to maintain a somewhat detached, relaxed attitude throughout what used to be tension-arousing aspects of flying.

There are also specialized instrumentation techniques, called "biofeedback," in which you actually can monitor the degree to which you achieve muscle relaxation and temperature control. These devices function much like a thermostat. Once they are attached to you, they constantly measure muscle tension and temperature, giving you a steady flow of information about your own ability to control inner tension. Biofeedback thus enables you to learn the steps to place yourself in a relaxed state.

Hypnosis and biofeedback require special equipment and training. Make sure you carefully examine the credentials of a prospective therapist before deciding to embark on this type of treatment.

Psychotherapy

Psychotherapy is a method of treatment aimed at exploring your unconscious fear and thus reducing the overall level of anxiety. It is a skill used by psychologists, psychiatrists, social workers, and other licensed, clinical counselors. Before entering into this therapeutic alliance, you must carefully assess not only the prospective therapist's training, but also whether this more probing, lengthy — and consequently more expensive — treatment is necessary to resolve the problem. If indicated, then, you and the therapist would begin an exploration of the underlying conflicts and fears that contribute to your phobia. You would discuss early experiences and feelings within the context of current relationships, until your choice of a phobic situation (i.e., flying) is better understood and then resolved.

Psychotherapy is best accomplished in individual treatment, where confidentiality and trust can be maximized.

Group therapy

Recently, there has been increased interest in group therapy as a vehicle for treating aerophobia. In this setting, you and the other members share common experiences, learn that your fears are not unique, and share ways of coping effectively. A group also is valuable as you try out your newly learned skills and feel the support of the other members. Group work is most beneficial for ongoing support; for psychotherapy, however, individual work ordinarily is the treatment of choice.

The Client-Therapist Relationship

Depending on how entrenched your fear is and how open you are to suggestion and relaxation, your treatment process may be as brief as five or six sessions or as long as it takes to analyze your fear. A competent therapist will be able to evaluate your situation comprehensively and make an appropriate recommendation. Your responsibility here is to assure yourself that you are working with an experienced, well-trained therapist. Many therapists, with training in an array of different disciplines, can administer behavior therapy; the issues for you are that you feel comfortable with your therapist, you feel a sense of confidence in talking with him or her, and you are assured of his or her ability to be helpful.

Whichever professional you use, you have the right to know if your values and the therapist's values are compatible. Initiate a frank discussion of your responsibilities and the therapist's responsibilities. Make sure you understand the nature of the therapy and rules about confidentiality. Discuss the different treatment options available, and be sure you feel comfortable with the process chosen. If you wish a second opinion, your therapist should welcome the request.

Specifically, you should pose the following questions to the prospective therapist before entering into an arrangement to begin treatment:
• What are your credentials?
• Are you licensed or certified to practice independently?

- What kind of experience have you had in treating aerophobia?
- What do you estimate to be the length of treatment?
- How often will you want to see me?
- What is the length of each session?
- What is your policy regarding phone calls? Can I call you at the office or at home if the need arises?
- If you are out of town, is there someone else I can call in an emergency?
- What is the charge per session?
- Will my health insurance cover part or all of the fee?
- Do you charge for a missed or canceled session?
- Will I be billed, or am I expected to pay the noninsured portion of the charge after each session?

Results

The success rate for the treatment processes described above is very high; almost everyone experiences at least some alleviation of anxiety. If you have not achieved some measure of relief after six to eight sessions, or do not feel that you're making progress, you should explore a different treatment option or seek a second opinion.

Whom To Contact

If you have trouble getting the name of a therapist from your family physician, local psychological or psychiatric groups, university departments, or community mental health clinic, check these publications at the library: the *National Register of Health Service Providers*, the *Register of Clinical Social Workers*, or the current directories for the American Psychological Association or the American Psychiatric Association. You can also contact the following organizations for general information, as well as names of practitioners in your area:

American Psychological
   Association
750 First Street N.E.
Washington, D.C. 20002
(202) 336-5500

Association for Advance-
   ment of Behavior Therapy
15 W. 36th Street
New York, NY 10018
(212) 279-7970

American Psychiatric
   Association
1400 K Street N.W.
Washington, D.C. 20005
(202) 682-6000

Anxiety Disorders
   Association of America
   (formerly the Phobia
   Society of America)
6000 Executive Blvd.
Suite 513
Rockville, MD 20852
(301) 231-9350

Murray E. Tieger, Ph.D., is Director of Psychology at the Jewish Hospital of Cincinnati and Associate Clinical Professor of Psychology at the University of Cincinnati and at the university's Medical College. Dr. Tieger specializes in group and individual psychotherapy. He has been in private practice for 36 years.

3

FEAR OF FLYING PROGRAMS

3

Fear of Flying Programs

This section is composed of more than 35 recognized programs that exist to help you overcome your fear. Unlike Section Two, "Finding Professional Help," which focuses on helping you find a qualified therapist who will work one-on-one with you or in a group, this section looks at systemized programs that were created specifically for aerophobics, using many of the same therapeutic methods discussed in Section Two. Before you begin to read about these programs, we urge you to review Section Two; it will define many of the disciplines and treatment techniques used to describe the programs in this section.

We have arranged the programs by geographic region, so you can easily see what's available in your area. Some programs are offered in multiple locations; others, although based in a particular city, will travel to your community if sufficient demand exists. See programs listed under "Multiple Locations" and those on pages 117, 119, 127, and 135. If there is no program listed near where you live, you can contact these programs to see if they could come to your area.

The programs listed here span numerous formats: seminars, structured support groups, individualized treatment, lectures, and hands-on workshops. They are sponsored by everything from private clinics to airlines to universities to not-for-profit organizations. Most are designed with a two-pronged approach, integrating anxiety management with aviation education. The success rates quoted were provided by those offering the services, and we regard them as honest results; however, keep in mind that criteria for measuring success can vary widely from program to program, and the differences in percentages can say as much about the yardstick used to measure them as they do about the quality of the program itself.

The cost of services are accurate as of this printing but are subject to change. If the program you're interested in is offered by a private clinic or other mental health facility, its cost may be offset by your medical insurance. Check your policy, or ask at the clinic.

Multiple Locations

Program:
AAir Born Fearless Flyer Program

WHERE:

The program is offered at major airports around the country. Locations may vary from year to year; check with American Airlines to see if a city near you has an upcoming seminar scheduled. Locations include the following metropolitan areas: **Greater New York, at Islip-Long Island, La Guardia, and Newark; San Jose and Orange County, California; Chicago/Milwaukee; Hartford, Connecticut; Raleigh/Durham; Toronto/ Buffalo; Nashville; Boston; Dallas-Ft. Worth; Detroit; Los Angeles; Washington, D.C./Baltimore; Philadelphia; and Miami, Florida.**

WHEN:

The two-day seminar is offered 45 times per year. Each day lasts eight to nine hours.

SPONSORSHIP AND INSTRUCTION:

AAir Born seminars are a project of American Airlines. The program is conducted by mental health professionals and American Airline pilots with more than 20 years of flying experience.

COST:

Up to 30 days prior to the program, the seminar costs $365; within 30 days, the fee is $415. The price includes an optional round-trip graduation flight.

REGISTRATION:

For information or a registration application, call (800) 451-5106 or (817) 967-4194, or fax to (817) 967-4003.

You can also write:
AAir Born
American Airlines Learning Center
Mail Drop 906
P.O. Box 619618
Dallas-Ft. Worth Airport, TX 75261-9618

ABOUT THE PROGRAM:

AAir Born seminars began in 1989 and have served some 2,200 people. The program encourages group support and teaches methods to break the cycle of fear and panic. Participants learn strategies for handling not only the fear of flying, but other fears that contribute to it, such as fear of heights, of falling, of enclosed spaces, and of losing control. Program leaders focus on anxiety-reducing techniques, including breathing skills, visualization, and creative imagery.

The seminar features opportunities to ask questions of crew members regarding the airline industry, safety and maintenance, special noises and activities of flight, and weather. Participants tour the cockpit and cabin of a stationary plane and are offered the opportunity to go on a graduation flight.

ABOUT THE RESULTS:

Follow-up studies have indicated a 93 percent success rate, based on how many seminar clients elect to take the graduation flight.

PROGRAM:

AOPA Air Safety Foundation's "Pinch-Hitter Course"

WHERE:

At various locations throughout the United States. The program is available at one time or another in most geographic regions of the country.

WHEN:

The course is taught about 45 times per year. Flight instruction is arranged individually.

SPONSORSHIP AND INSTRUCTION:

The program is sponsored by the AOPA Air Safety Foundation, a not-for-profit safety education organization. Ground school and flight instruction are taught by AOPA flight instructors.

COST:

$395. A manual, which is included in the cost of the program, is also for sale separately for $6.50.

REGISTRATION:

Call the AOPA Air Safety Foundation at (800) 638-3010 or (301) 695-2170.

ABOUT THE PROGRAM:

The Air Safety Foundation promotes pilot safety by offering a series of refresher courses. The Pinch-Hitter Course is its only course for nonpilots; it focuses on helping nonpilots understand and enjoy flying, and prepares them to take over in an emergency.

The ground school portion of the course is a four-hour lesson in flight control, instruments, navigation, and emergency procedures. The accompanying manual reinforces material taught in the class. After students complete the ground school, they arrange through the Air Safety Foundation for four hours of flight instruction. The foundation finds an instructor in the student's area to provide the training.

ABOUT THE RESULTS:

The foundation reports a "very high" success rate. In addition to educating and empowering nonpilots, a significant number of participants go on to get their pilot's license.

PROGRAM:
How to Conquer Fear of Flying:
A Self-Help Program

WHERE:

The program is regularly scheduled in **New York/New Jersey, Chicago, San Diego, Denver, Los Angeles, West Palm Beach, Toronto,** and **Ottawa.** However, it will travel to any location in the United States or Canada where five to ten people have signed up for it. The seminar takes place at major airport hotels and airline terminals, as well as corporate training facilities.

WHEN:

This is a one-day seminar, conducted throughout the year on either Saturdays or Sundays, from 9 A.M. to 6 P.M.

SPONSORSHIP AND INSTRUCTION:

The program is sponsored by the Pegasus Fear of Flying Foundation, Inc., a not-for-profit corporation established to support and promote legitimate efforts to conquer aerophobia. In addition to the seminars for aerophobics, the foundation provides training for therapists, flight and cabin crew members, travel agents, and corporate travel departments; it also offers VIP services for high-profile aerophobics. The foundation works with the help of a counseling board, composed of eleven noted clinical psychologists from around the country.

Pegasus was established by its president, Captain David A. Linsley, who has taught fear of flying seminars since 1969. Captain Linsley is a commercial airline pilot and former naval aviation flight and ground school instructor.

COST:

The seminar costs $350, which is considered a tax-deductible donation. Anyone who organizes five to ten people for a seminar gets his or her cost waived. Captain Linsley recommends that people first try to overcome their fear by buying, for $25, the text from which the seminar is taught. If they then decide to take the seminar, the price of the text is deducted.

REGISTRATION:

Call (800) FEAR NOT (332-7668) for information, or write to the foundation at the following address:

Pegasus Fear of Flying Foundation
301-B 53rd Street
West Palm Beach, FL 33407

ABOUT THE PROGRAM:

Group sizes are limited to ten participants, to ensure individualized attention. The seminar consists of nine hours of intensive training, focusing on instruction by teams of airline pilots and psychologists. The groups progress from the classroom to the airport terminal to the aircraft. Breakfast, lunch, and a congratulatory champagne toast are provided. There is no graduation flight.

Follow-up services offer graduate feedback via the foundation's 800 telephone number; counseling advice; and attendance at subsequent seminars at no additional cost.

ABOUT THE RESULTS:

Pegasus reports that it has graduated more than 600 participants with a higher than 99 percent success rate—only four have not been successful at overcoming their fear. The foundation offers a money-back guarantee.

This program has been featured in various mediums, including NBC's "Today Show" and CNBC's "Dick Cavett Show."

PROGRAM:

The Program for the Fearful Flyer

WHERE:

The program travels to areas where the demand is high. It has been available in most major cities in the United States, as well as in London.

WHEN:

Groups are scheduled whenever enough people are interested in signing up. They also are organized for universities or corporate groups upon request. A typical seminar would meet for four three-hour evenings.

SPONSORSHIP AND INSTRUCTION:

The program was developed for Pan American Airways by Captain T.W. Cummings. Captain Cummings directs the program with help from two seminar leaders, who have more than 15 years of experience in treating aerophobia. Carmen Cummings, who has an M.A. in Counseling Psychology, is Assistant Director.

COST:

The seminar costs $300, which includes an accompanying booklet and two audiotapes. Air fare for the graduation flight varies. The booklet and tapes can be purchased as a separate package for $28.

REGISTRATION:

Call (305) 261-7042 to register interest and to receive information about the program, or write to:

Captain T.W. Cummings, President
The Program for the Fearful Flyer
2021 Country Club Prado
Coral Gables, FL 33134

If a seminar is to be held in your area, you will be notified three to four weeks in advance.

ABOUT THE PROGRAM:

The Program for the Fearful Flyer was developed in 1974, when Captain Cummings was a pilot with Pan American. Since then, he has held seminars across the country for all the major airlines, as well as many other groups. Participants number in the thousands.

As a prerequisite to the group meetings, participants are asked to prepare with a booklet, "Answers to 75 Questions About Flight and About Fear," and two audiotapes. One tape teaches the program's relaxation method; the other details the airport and flight experience.

The group seminars, which are limited to 12 participants, involve lectures, aircraft tours, and open discussions about flight and the feelings that accompany it. At least one of the sessions meets at the airport and is conducted on a parked jet. There is also a graduation flight.

Personal counseling is available without charge during the course of the program. For example, a participant who is claustrophobic in addition to being aerophobic is given individual attention to overcome both barriers.

ABOUT THE RESULTS:

More than 90 percent of the program's participants go on the graduation flight.

This program, which is one of the earliest developed for aerophobics, has been widely recognized for its results. Publications that have given it favorable reviews include *People* magazine, the *San Francisco Examiner*, the *New York Times*, the *Chicago Tribune*, the *Los Angeles Times*, *Psychology Today*, *Time*, *Air Transport World*, and *U.S. News and World Report*. Most major U.S. television networks have covered the seminars, and BBC-TV in London broadcast a 30-minute feature on the program.

PROGRAM:
USAir Fearful Flyers Program

WHERE:

As of this printing, the program is available in **Los Angeles; San Diego; Baltimore; Pittsburgh; Charlotte, North Carolina; Rochester, New York; Boston; Washington, D.C.; Philadelphia;** and **Indianapolis.** Other cities are sometimes added, however, so check with a local USAir office to see if it's coming to your area. All classes are held at the cities' major airports.

WHEN:

The course consists of seven three-hour sessions, meeting one night per week for seven weeks. It is offered yearly in each of ten metropolitan areas.

SPONSORSHIP AND INSTRUCTION:

The program was developed for USAir by Carol Stauffer, a clinical social worker and certified group psychotherapist. She codirects the program with Captain Frank Petee, a pilot with 40 years of commercial flying experience and USAir's former Director of Flight Training. The two also coauthored a book, *Fly Without Fear,* based on the principles of the program.

COST:

$295, which includes the accompanying book and audiotape, as well as the one-hour graduation flight. Also, each participant can bring a guest on the flight free of charge.

REGISTRATION:

Write to the following address:

USAir Fearful Flyers Program
P.O. Box 100
Glenshaw, PA 15101

ABOUT THE PROGRAM:

The Fearful Flyers Program was developed in 1975. Since then, it has served more than 5,000 people and has won the National Travel Industry Award.

The program offers an interwoven approach of aviation education and relaxation training. Captain Petee discusses topics such as pilot training, flight preparations, en route flight operations, and safety procedures. USAir maintenance personnel talk about airplane maintenance, and flight attendants discuss their training. An FAA representative leads a tour of the control tower and radar room.

Several meetings are held on board an aircraft, where students explore the cabin and cockpit. During one meeting, the class taxis around the airfield without taking off. The last class is a one-hour flight.

Throughout the seven weeks of classes, Ms. Stauffer teaches and reinforces relaxation techniques. Each person is given a tape of relaxation exercises and is expected to practice between classes. She also teaches thought-stopping as a way of managing anxiety.

ABOUT THE RESULTS:

USAir conducted a research project to track program participants since 1975. The study showed that 95 percent of the respondents were still flying or planning trips. In addition, the average anxiety level about flying had dropped from "extremely anxious" to "relatively calm."

PROGRAM:
Delta Fearful Flyers Program

Another resource to look for comes from Delta Air Lines. Delta had a comprehensive program for aerophobics in Atlanta for 17 years. The program is now on hold while the company evaluates the merits of expanding or modifying it. In the interim, Delta will mail an informational packet free of charge to anyone who inquires about fear of flying programs. The packet, which typically consists of articles of interest to the fearful flyer, is continuously updated.

To receive the packet or to obtain current information about the status of the program, contact Delta's Public Relations Department at (404) 715-5162.

EAST

MARYLAND/WASHINGTON, D.C.

PROGRAM:
Center for Behavioral Medicine
"Fear of Flying" class

WHERE:

The group meets at the Center for Behavioral Medicine in Baltimore, with two of the sessions held at Baltimore-Washington International Airport.

WHEN:

Groups are scheduled periodically, whenever five to eight participants have registered. The program consists of ten sessions.

SPONSORSHIP AND INSTRUCTION:

Classes are taught by David A. Poleno, a licensed therapist with nine years of experience specializing in phobia treatment.

COST:

$600, plus the cost of the participant's air fare and a portion of the therapist's ticket.

REGISTRATION:

Enroll by calling (410) 764-7462, or write to:
> Center for Behavioral Medicine
> "Fear of Flying"
> 7238 T Park Heights Ave.
> Baltimore, MD 21208

ABOUT THE PROGRAM:

The program explains phobia and uses cognitive and behavioral therapy to manage fear. It also uses in-vivo techniques. Participants spend two two-hour sessions at the airport, where they board a plane and meet with a pilot who explains the sounds and functions of an airplane.

ABOUT THE RESULTS:

The program reports that its success rate is approximately 93 percent.

PROGRAM:

Center for Behavioral Medicine's Phobia/Panic Disorder Program

WHERE:

The program serves the Bethesda, Maryland area.

WHEN:

Groups are organized when the need demands, approximately two to three times per year. They run for four to eight sessions. Individual treatment is available by appointment.

SPONSORSHIP AND INSTRUCTION:

The Center's Director is Brian J. Depenbrock, L.C.S.W., who has fifteen years of experience in treating anxiety disorders.

COST:

The program costs $65 per person per session, plus the cost of a graduation flight. Individual sessions cost $85.

REGISTRATION:

Call (301) 656-9454 to arrange for an evaluation session, or write to:

Center for Behavioral Medicine
4520 East West Highway
Suite 510
Bethesda, MD 20814

ABOUT THE PROGRAM:

The Center has been treating anxiety disorders for 20 years. It has a structured 16-week program for phobia and panic disorder; the four- to eight-week program for fearful flyers is a condensed version of that program.

Participants first must arrange for an individual evaluation session. Medication is prescribed when indicated. Groups are formed when four or five people have signed up for the program.

Treatment concentrates on cognitive and behavioral techniques and relaxation exercises. It also involves in-vivo exposure and, increasingly, hypnotherapy. The program culminates with a graduation flight.

ABOUT THE RESULTS:

The program reports a success rate of approximately 75 percent.

MASSACHUSETTS

PROGRAM:

Exposure Therapy and Counseling Services

WHERE:

In West Springfield, Massachusetts, with one session meeting at Bradley Field Airport in Windsor Locks, Connecticut.

WHEN:

By appointment. The client must start the program at least four weeks prior to a planned flight.

SPONSORSHIP AND INSTRUCTION:

The program is directed by Cynthia Szela, L.C.S.W., who has specialized for ten years in phobias, panic disorder, and agoraphobia.

COST:

$60 per one-hour session, or $240 for the four-session program.

REGISTRATION:

Call (413) 733-2034 to set up an appointment, or write to:

Cynthia Szela, Director
Exposure Therapy and Counseling Services
201 Park Ave.
West Springfield, MA 01089

ABOUT THE PROGRAM:

Ms. Szela works one-on-one with highly motivated clients: fearful flyers who have already booked a flight. She prefers to meet with participants for one session per week for four weeks prior to the flight.

The program focuses on cognitive and behavioral treatment combined with in-vivo exposure. Participants are taught coping skills and techniques to manage and control anxiety. The final session exposes the participant to the airport, where she or he boards a plane and goes through the learned techniques and skills. Clients are provided a tape to educate and reinforce materials taught in the classes.

ABOUT THE RESULTS:

The program reports a 99 percent success rate.

PROGRAM:

Fearless Flying: The Complete Program for Relaxed Air Travel

WHERE:

The program is offered in the Boston area, at the Institute for Psychology of Air Travel and at Logan Airport.

WHEN:

The ten-week group therapy program is available five times per year. Optional programs—private therapy, on-site workshops for industry, and a home-study course—are arranged as needed.

SPONSORSHIP AND INSTRUCTION:

Fearless Flying is sponsored by the Institute for Psychology of Air Travel and directed by Albert G. Forgione, Ph.D., a specialist in aerophobia since 1972. He conducts the course with the help of two assistants, as well as guest speakers from the aviation industry.

COST:

The group program costs $300, which includes an accompanying book and a four-cassette audiotape series. The $300 also entitles participants to lifetime privileges of booster sessions or retaking the course. The other program options cost: $90 per hour for three to four individual therapy sessions; $90 per person for on-site industry workshops; and $59.95 post-paid for the home-study course, which includes the book, the audiotapes, and an instructional booklet.

REGISTRATION:

Call the Institute at (617) 437-1811, or write:

Institute for Psychology of Air Travel
Suite 300
25 Huntington Ave.
Boston, MA 02116

You can obtain the home-study course by sending a $59.95 check to the above address.

ABOUT THE PROGRAM:

Fearless Flying has been in continuous service since 1972. Group treatment involves progressive muscle relaxation, diaphragmatic breathing techniques, cognitive/behavioral therapy, antistress coping maneuvers, and nutritional counseling. Participants also learn acupressure techniques for relaxation and tension control. Aviation education is provided by a tour of the airport, question-and-answer sessions with a pilot, and two classes conducted on a parked plane. A graduation flight is optional.

Each of the four audiotapes deals with a particular aspect of aerophobia. One concentrates on relaxation exercises, a general discussion of anxiety and fear, and the nature of air travel fear and coping techniques. It includes sounds of an actual flight. Another tape features a retired Pan American pilot with 30 years of flying experience answering typical questions posed by phobics. The third tape has an individually guided relaxation exercise taped on an actual flight; it also has former phobics talking about their fears and successes. The fourth tape reiterates the relaxation exercises and discusses antistress lifestyles.

ABOUT THE RESULTS:

The program's brochure relates several statements of recommendation, including quotations from NBC's "Today Show" and CBS radio.

PROGRAM:
Upward Bound Fearful Flyers Program

WHERE:

Upward Bound is available in the eastern Massachusetts area. Group sessions are conducted at the Anxiety and Phobia Center, with two trips to Boston's Logan Airport.

WHEN:

The program is offered six times yearly, with individual and crisis sessions available as needed. Regular sessions meet weekly for two hours per night over five weeks; the sixth session is a graduation flight.

SPONSORSHIP AND INSTRUCTION:

The program and the Anxiety and Phobia Center are directed by Richard C. Raynard, Ph.D. Dr. Raynard has specialized in phobias and related fears for 20 years.

COST:

$300, plus round-trip air fare, which usually costs between $125 and $150.

REGISTRATION:

Enroll by calling (617) 659-2111 and asking for a brochure and registration form. You can also write:

Anxiety and Phobia Center
320 Washington Street
Norwell, MA 02061

ABOUT THE PROGRAM:

Upward Bound features 16 calming methods, relaxation training being only one. Participants receive a computerized phobia assessment and are taught how to handle worry and anticipatory anxiety. Their training in aerodynamics and air safety includes pilot guest speakers, visits to the airport, and two simulated flights. The graduation flight is a round trip to New York on a regularly scheduled commercial flight.

The program also offers partner training, to enlist support from the phobic's family.

ABOUT THE RESULTS:

An independent study conducted by a Boston university showed 94 percent of those completing the program go on to fly in comfort.

NEW YORK

PROGRAM:
Marvin L. Aronson, Ph.D.

WHERE:

Treatment is available in Manhattan and Mt. Vernon, New York.

WHEN:

By appointment. Individual therapy ranges from one to fifteen sessions; group therapy ranges from eight to fifteen sessions, depending on the needs of participants.

SPONSORSHIP AND INSTRUCTION:

Treatment is by Dr. Marvin Aronson, clinical psychologist and Director of Group Therapy at the Postgraduate Center for Mental Health in New York City. Dr. Aronson has worked in the field of aerophobia for more than 20 years.

COST:

Individual sessions are billed at between $100 and $125. Group sessions cost $60 to $75.

REGISTRATION:

Call (212) 532-2135 or (914) 664-1326 to set up an appointment or to sign up for a group. Groups are formed with a minimum of three to four participants.

You can also write for more information:

Dr. Marvin L. Aronson
124 East 28th Street
New York, NY 10016

ABOUT THE PROGRAM:

Dr. Aronson utilizes a combined approach of psychodynamic, behavioral, and cognitive treatments, emphasizing any one of the three as individual participants require. He also provides in-vivo exposure and graduation flights when indicated, but sometimes leaves those steps to friends or relatives, who can become what he calls "therapeutic adjuncts."

ABOUT THE RESULTS:

For those who complete therapy, Dr. Aronson reports a 90 percent success rate.

PROGRAM:

Aviaphobia Seminars & Associates

WHERE:

As of this printing, the program is available in Long Island, New York, at MacArthur and Republic airports; in the New York City area at JFK and La Guardia airports; and in White Plains, New York, at Westchester Airport. Expansion plans include Newark, Chicago, Washington, D.C., and Dallas-Ft. Worth.

WHEN:

Four to five times a year, on a group appointment basis. The 36-hour program is taught over four weekend days; a shorter option is also available. In addition to class time, the program requires homework.

SPONSORSHIP AND INSTRUCTION:

ASA is headed by Chuck Blessing, who has 12 years in aerophobia research and development, as well as 25 years in aviation, including experience as a commercial pilot and aerospace engineer. He conducts the program in conjunction with a behavioral therapist and a psychologist/hypno-therapist.

COST:

$497, which includes books, tapes, instruction, counseling, graduation flight, and field trips.

REGISTRATION:

A $100 registration fee will enroll you in the course and will be applied toward the cost of the program. Call (516) 471-6105 for information, or write to:

Aviaphobia Seminars & Associates
344 Avenue B, Suite 100
Ronkonkoma, NY 11779

ABOUT THE PROGRAM:

ASA works with TWA and American Airlines. The company says it prides itself on getting the fearful flyer to actually enjoy flying, and offers its students a money-back guarantee.

The program follows this outline:

1. Education—overcoming the fear of the unknown
2. Lack of control—teaching confidence and desensitization/relaxation exercises
3. Meeting the players—field trips to airlines, the FAA, etc.
4. Hypnotherapy session—simulated flight experience
5. Positive thinking techniques/the "buddy support system"
6. Graduation flight—round-trip on a commercial jet aircraft to a nearby city

ABOUT THE RESULTS:

ASA claims a 97 percent success rate.

PROGRAM:
Focus: A Private Mental Health Center "Fearful Flyer" program

WHERE:

At the Albany County Airport in Albany, New York.

WHEN:

Group treatment is available for four weeks each fall. Individual treatment is by appointment.

SPONSORSHIP AND INSTRUCTION:

The program is run by Richard Platt, Ph.D., who has 20 years of clinical experience treating anxiety difficulties. He has directed the Fearful Flyer program since 1987.

COST:

$435, including the cost of materials and the graduation flight. Individual sessions are $75 apiece.

REGISTRATION:

Call (518) 482-8331 for information, or write:
Richard Platt, Ph.D.
"Fearful Flyer" program
346 Quail Street
Albany, NY 12208

ABOUT THE PROGRAM:

All classes are held at the airport. Participants are given reading materials covering information about safety, the mechanics of flight, and the sounds and motions that planes make. Aviation information is provided by a pilot. Participants tour the FAA tower and board and explore parked airplanes.

At the same time, participants learn about anxiety and are taught anxiety-reduction techniques. They practice those techniques during a simulated flight. The program also incorporates support from former aerophobics, group support, a round-trip graduation flight, and follow-up services.

Another feature of the program is that it encourages spouses or travel partners to participate in the classes. The partners receive information that can help the aerophobic when they fly post-program.

ABOUT THE RESULTS:

The program claims that 95 percent of the participants complete the graduation flight; 90 percent continue to fly post-program.

PROGRAM:
Travel & Fly Without Fear

WHERE:

In New York City, at La Guardia Airport.

WHEN:

The program is ongoing; it meets on Thursday nights, from 8 P.M. to 10 P.M.

SPONSORSHIP AND INSTRUCTION:

Travel & Fly Without Fear is directed by Carol Gross, who has been with the program for 20 years. She is a specialist in the field of phobias and has written articles for a variety of publications, including *Newsday* and the *New York Times*.

COST:

The program charges a one-year membership fee of $10. After that, the sessions are $30 each.

REGISTRATION:

Call (212) 697-6777 or fax to (212) 682-5230, or write to:
Carol Gross, Director
Travel & Fly Without Fear
310 Madison Ave.
New York, NY 10017

ABOUT THE PROGRAM:

This group program began in the early '70s and has served more than 5,000 participants. Although it doesn't consist of a set number of meetings, the average number of sessions per person is six.

Features of the program include guest speakers from both the aviation industry and the mental health profession—pilots, maintenance personnel, air traffic controllers, flight attendants, and psychologists. Participants visit the control tower, and the program culminates with a graduation flight.

ABOUT THE RESULTS:

The company doesn't conduct follow-up studies, but it reports a "high rate" of success.

PROGRAM:

White Plains Hospital Center's Phobia Program

WHERE:

In New York, at White Plains Hospital and either La Guardia Airport or Westchester Airport.

WHEN:

The program runs for five weeks. Groups specifically for aerophobics are arranged only occasionally; at other times, fearful flyers can join five-week groups that include people with other fears but which teach the same coping principles. There are also ongoing self-help groups available for a wide range of phobias.

SPONSORSHIP AND INSTRUCTION:

The phobia program is run by White Plains Hospital. It is headed by Director Fredric J. Neuman, M.D., and Director Emeritus Manuel D. Zane, M.D.

Dr. Zane developed what he termed "contextual therapy," which is the approach the phobia clinic employs. He began White Plains Hospital's first group phobia clinic in 1971. He is also the author of the book *Your Phobia: Understanding Your Fears Through Contextual Therapy.* Dr. Neuman has written numerous books, including *Fighting Fear: An Eight-Week Guide to Treating Your Own Phobias.*

COST:

$750, which includes a round-trip graduation flight to either Boston or Washington, D.C. Participation in the self-help groups costs $10 per session.

REGISTRATION:

Call (914) 681-1038, or write to the following:
White Plains Hospital Center
Phobia Program
Davis Avenue at Post Road
White Plains, NY 10601

ABOUT THE PROGRAM:

Contextual therapy is the treatment and study of a phobia in its actual setting. It is based on the following guidelines:

1. Expect and allow fear to arise and accept that you have a phobia.
2. When fear appears, wait.
3. Try to remain focused on things in the present.
4. Label your fear level 1-10 and watch it go up and down.
5. Do things that lower and keep manageable the level of fear.
6. Try to function with fear.

The five-week program begins with two sessions at White Plains Hospital, where participants learn the theory of contextual therapy. The next two sessions are held at one of the two area airports and may feature lectures by airline pilots. The last session is the graduation flight. Phobia aides, most of whom are former phobics who have trained under Dr. Zane's supervision, accompany participants on the flight.

If a fearful flyer needs a program to address his or her specific phobia at a time when the program doesn't have a group for fearful flyers under way, personnel will refer clients to other services.

ABOUT THE RESULTS:

Follow-up studies show that 96 percent of the clinic's treated clients—including those treated for phobias other than fear of flying—have been helped. For the 20 clients who have gone through the program specifically to treat aerophobia, all but one have taken the graduation flight.

PENNSYLVANIA

PROGRAM:

Simone Gorko, Psychologist

WHERE:

Suburbs of Philadelphia and Allentown, Pennsylvania.

WHEN:

By appointment. Treatment is one-on-one, and the length is determined by individual needs. Group therapy is available if a sufficient number of clients indicate interest.

SPONSORSHIP AND INSTRUCTION:

Treatment is administered by Simone Gorko, M.S., who herself survived an airplane crash. Ms. Gorko has been treating aerophobics for eight years.

COST:

$90 per one-hour session.

REGISTRATION:

Call (215) 667-7999 for an appointment or write for more information:

Simone Gorko, M.S.
822 Montgomery Ave.
Suite 314
Narberth, PA 19072

ABOUT THE PROGRAM:

Treatment begins with individual assessment of the nature of the phobia. What follows may include relaxation training, cognitive therapy, hypnosis, desensitization, and accompanying the client on a flight.

ABOUT THE RESULTS:

Ms. Gorko reports that every aerophobic she has ever worked with has successfully flown.

SOUTH

FLORIDA

PROGRAM:

Anxiety-Phobia Unit, Family Centered Counseling

WHERE:

Palm Beach County, Florida.

WHEN:

The program is available whenever four to ten people register.

SPONSORSHIP AND INSTRUCTION:

Treatment is by John Skow, Ph.D., L.C.S.W. Dr. Skow has specialized in phobias, fears, anxiety, and panic attacks since 1975; he first began holding groups for aerophobics in 1980.

COST:

$80 per one-hour session, with most groups running for six sessions.

REGISTRATION:

Call (407) 736-1340, or write:
John Skow, Ph.D.
2828 South Seacrest Blvd. #212
Boynton Beach, FL 33435

ABOUT THE PROGRAM:

Methods include cognitive/behavioral treatment, desensitization, relaxation exercises, panic control, and gradual exposure techniques. The program usually uses office simulation rather than trips to the airport or experience on a plane.

103

ABOUT THE RESULTS:

Dr. Skow reports that participants have been "very pleased" with the treatment.

NORTH CAROLINA

PROGRAM:

Phobia Treatment Center of the Triad
"Fearless Flying" program

WHERE:

In Greensboro, North Carolina, at the Piedmont Triad International Airport.

WHEN:

Groups are organized whenever the need demands. This is a six-week program, meeting one evening per week for five weeks and ending with a graduation flight on a Saturday or Sunday. Individual treatment is available by appointment.

SPONSORSHIP AND INSTRUCTION:

The program is run by Beverly Lawrenson, who has specialized in desensitization therapy for 12 years.

COST:

$185, plus air fare for the graduation flight.

REGISTRATION:

Call (919) 292-6947, or write:
Beverly Lawrenson
Phobia Treatment Center of the Triad, Inc.
5318 W. Friendly Ave.
Greensboro, NC 27410

ABOUT THE PROGRAM:

This program emphasizes systematic desensitization. To maximize exposure, all classes are held at the airport. Participants tour maintenance operations, air school facilities, the airport, and an airplane. They speak with pilots and flight attendants, and hear guest lecturers discuss various air traffic topics. A flight simulator gives participants some flight experience, and they practice relaxation exercises during the simulation and also while sitting inside a stationary plane. The program ends with an optional graduation flight.

ABOUT THE RESULTS:

The program reports a 100 percent success rate.

VIRGINIA

PROGRAM:

Roundhouse Fearless Flying Program

WHERE:

At the Roundhouse Square Counseling Center in Alexandria, Virginia.

WHEN:

Groups are organized when there is adequate demand. They generally meet for five sessions.

SPONSORSHIP AND INSTRUCTION:

The program director is Burton J. Rubin, a specialist in behavioral skills training and desensitization.

COST:

$350 plus the cost of a graduation flight. There may be additional fees if medication is indicated. Individual therapy is available at $90 per session.

REGISTRATION:

Call (703) 836-7130 and ask to speak to the intake coordinator, or write:

Roundhouse Fearless Flying Program
1444 Duke Street
Alexandria, VA 22314

ABOUT THE PROGRAM:

Therapy involves educational, cognitive, behavioral, and supportive elements, together with medication when indicated. Group sessions include guest lecturers with expertise in aviation and air traffic control. There may also be speakers who address biological factors involved with aerophobia. The group program concludes with a graduation flight; individual therapy concludes with a videotape simulation.

ABOUT THE RESULTS:

The program reports a high degree of client satisfaction, with a high percentage participating in the graduation flight.

SOUTHWEST

ARIZONA

PROGRAM:
Cleared for Takeoff

WHERE:
Sky Harbor International Airport, Phoenix, Arizona.

WHEN:
The first Thursday of each month, from 7 P.M. to 9 P.M.

SPONSORSHIP AND INSTRUCTION:
Sponsored by Sky Harbor International Airport; taught by John A. Moran, Ph.D., P.C.

COST:
$20 per meeting.

REGISTRATION:
Call Dr. Moran's office at (602) 946-0801, or fax to (602) 946-0814. You can also register at the door without advance notice.

ABOUT THE PROGRAM:
Cleared for Takeoff has a drop-in policy, so participants can attend as many or as few sessions as they desire.

Each month there is a different guest lecturer who teaches with Dr. Moran. The lecturers' backgrounds alternate: One month will feature a mental health expert, the next month will feature an airlines professional. The first hour is devoted to an informational presentation about either anxiety management or aviation. The second hour takes place

109

in a parked airplane, where participants can become familiar with the surroundings, learn about the plane, and participate in group discussions and question-and-answer sessions.

For participants who are interested, Dr. Moran is available for one-on-one instruction during a flight.

RESULTS:

Dr. Moran does not conduct follow-up studies but is pleased with his clients' results.

PROGRAM:
Randall J. Garland, Ph.D.

WHERE:

At the Tucson International Airport in Tucson, Arizona. Additional treatment is available at Dr. Garland's office.

WHEN:

The airport program is available twice a year and consists of a two-hour lecture workshop. Individual sessions are available by appointment.

SPONSORSHIP AND INSTRUCTION:

Dr. Garland is a specialist in anxiety disorders. He has trained under George Mayo, Ph.D., who also specializes in anxiety disorders. Dr. Mayo has produced an audiotape, "Ready for Takeoff."

COST:

$30 for the workshop.

REGISTRATION:

Call (602) 887-0993, or write:
Randall J. Garland, Ph.D.
4760 North Oracle Road
Suite 200
Tucson, AZ 85705

ABOUT THE PROGRAM:

The workshop features education via guest speakers and an airport visit; relaxation exercises; and various methods of exposure—including boarding a plane—to reduce fear. It also offers group support and self-help materials, such as books, audiotapes, and videotapes.

ABOUT THE RESULTS:

Approximately 70 percent of the participants show a marked improvement according to Dr. Garland.

TEXAS

PROGRAM:

Anxiety, Mood, and Phobia Center

WHERE:

In Ft. Worth, Texas, at the phobia center and Dallas-Ft. Worth Airport.

WHEN:

Phobia support groups are ongoing. Individual sessions and home visits are by appointment. The length of treatment runs from 12 to 20 sessions.

SPONSORSHIP AND INSTRUCTION:

The phobia center is directed by anxiety disorder specialists Carolyn Self, Ph.D., and Sam Barklis, M.D. Dr. Self has conducted a $10,000 study on panic attacks, funded by the Upjohn Company.

COST:

$75 per group session, including audiotapes and reading materials. Individual sessions cost $100.

REGISTRATION:

You can drop in to a support group; call (817) 335-FEAR (3327) to find out when they're held. You can also call to obtain an informational packet or to set up an appointment. Or write:

> Anxiety, Mood, and Phobia Center
> 1612 Summit
> Suite 240
> Ft. Worth, TX 76102

ABOUT THE PROGRAM:

The phobia center's groups combine aerophobics with other phobics and put them through a structured, hierarchical program.

In-vivo outings are to the local airport, where each group member is assigned a task that challenges his or her skills. For example, while the aerophobic is being exposed to the airplane, the member who suffers from driving phobia drives to the airport, and the member who suffers from social phobia must ask a stranger for assistance.

Besides in-vivo exposure, therapy includes education about anxiety and the development of phobias and depression; cognitive restructuring; breathing and relaxation exercises; goal-setting; and medication when necessary.

ABOUT THE RESULTS:

The center carefully measures its success rate according to three criteria: depression, anxiety, and behavior. Based on improvement in those areas, the program reports that approximately 84 percent of clients who finish the group enjoy an 85 percent improvement of symptoms.

MIDWEST

ILLINOIS

PROGRAM:

Agoraphobia and Anxiety Treatment Center "Fear of Flying" program

WHERE:

In Arlington Heights, Illinois, serving the Greater Chicago area.

WHEN:

Groups are offered approximately every two months and run from four to eight sessions.

SPONSORSHIP AND INSTRUCTION:

The program has been taught since 1988 by Marleen Lorenz, R.N., M.A., and Chris Louro, M.A., M.S., both specialists in treating phobias, panic, and anxiety disorders. Ms. Lorenz herself is a recovered aerophobic.

COST:

$70 per session, either group or individual.

REGISTRATION:

Call (708) 577-8809 for an appointment or additional information, or write:

Agoraphobia and Anxiety Treatment Center
    "Fear of Flying" program
    3265 N. Arlington Heights Road, #304
    Arlington Heights, IL 60004

ABOUT THE PROGRAM:

The program offers services and support in the following areas:

1. Education regarding the safety of air travel. This includes mechanical factors, air traffic control, weather conditions, and airline personnel compliance issues.
2. Skills training in relaxation techniques and anxiety/panic management.
3. Cognitive techniques to change attitudes about flying.
4. A visit to the airport and a meeting with a pilot.
5. A graduation flight.
6. Additional practice flights.
7. Follow-up support groups.

ABOUT THE RESULTS:

On follow-up studies, 90 percent of clients flew at least once after completing the program.

PROGRAM:
Phobicare

WHERE:

The program is based in Orland Park, Illinois, and is available at six locations in the Chicago area. It also will travel to other locations for a group.

WHEN:

Groups are scheduled by appointment. They consist of six classes plus a graduation flight.

SPONSORSHIP AND INSTRUCTION:

The program is taught by Dr. Gilbert R. Parent and also includes the services of psychiatrists and social workers. Dr. Parent has been involved in the research and treatment of aerophobia since 1978.

COST:

$510, plus the cost of a round-trip graduation flight.

REGISTRATION:

Call Dr. Parent at (800) 682-1182 or (708) 403-3233, or call his beeper at (708) 953-3941. Or write:

> Dr. Gilbert Parent
> 60 Orland Square Drive
> Suite 2
> Orland Park, IL 60462

ABOUT THE PROGRAM:

This program focuses on the individual within a group context and promises to work with each participant until the problem with flying is resolved.

Dr. Parent's six-week class includes a visit to a small airport. He customizes an audiotape for each individual

117

based on his or her specific needs. The course concludes with Dr. Parent leading an overnight round-trip flight.

ABOUT THE RESULTS:

To date, Dr. Parent reports that 100 percent of the 141 participants have progressed to the graduation flight.

KANSAS

PROGRAM:

The Joy of Flying: Overcoming the Fear

WHERE:

The program is based at Kansas University Medical Center in Kansas City, Kansas, but it travels to any location with a minimum of ten participants.

WHEN:

Groups are organized as the need demands.

SPONSORSHIP AND INSTRUCTION:

The program is taught by Walter H. Gunn, Ph.D., an aviation psychologist who is also a retired airline captain. Dr. Gunn has 39 years and 29,000 hours of flight experience. He's written a book, *The Joy of Flying: Overcoming the Fear*, and is an Assistant Professor of Clinical Psychiatry and Adjunct Professor of Aviation Human Factors.

COST:

Groups meeting at Kansas University Medical Center cost $90 per person for a one-day seminar. Those meeting at other locations cost $90 plus expenses for travel, meals, and lodging. The program is available free of charge for a spouse or travel companion.

REGISTRATION:

Call (913) 588-6493, or write to:
W.H. Gunn, Ph.D.
Kansas University Medical Center
39th and Rainbow Blvd.
Kansas City, Kansas 66160

ABOUT THE PROGRAM:

The Joy of Flying focuses on personality factors that contribute to aerophobia. Dr. Gunn uses a combined approach of cognitive/behavioral and rational/emotional therapy principles. He also emphasizes technical aspects of flight, based on anecdotes and experiences garnered from his flying career.

Dr. Gunn also provides one-on-one counseling, which requires two to three sessions, plus practice procedures to follow with a support person.

ABOUT THE RESULTS:

Dr. Gunn reports an 80 percent success rate.

MISSOURI

PROGRAM:

Mid-County Psychological Associates "Freedom to Fly" program

WHERE:

In St. Louis, Missouri, with sessions at the Mid-County office and at Lambert International Airport.

WHEN:

Groups are organized up to twice yearly. They consist of six two-and-a-half-hour weekly sessions.

SPONSORSHIP AND INSTRUCTION:

The program is conducted by Ronald Scott, Ph.D., a former professor now in private practice. Dr. Scott, who has a specialty in anxiety, began his Freedom to Fly groups in 1984.

COST:

Participation in the group costs $300 plus the cost of the graduation flight, which usually is based on group rates. Individual sessions are $85 per hour.

REGISTRATION:

Call (314) 997-8877 to enroll in the program or to be notified when a group is scheduled. Or write:

Dr. Ronald Scott
Mid-County Psychological Associates
777 S. New Ballas Road, Suite 129W
St. Louis, MO 63141

ABOUT THE PROGRAM:

Freedom to Fly enjoys a cooperative relationship with Lambert International Airport and TWA Air Lines.

121

Groups consist of between five and twelve people. Participants receive information about airplanes, airlines, and anxieties, and they're taught cognitive and behavioral anxiety-management skills. A gradual desensitization approach includes sessions at the airport, opportunities to board aircraft, and conversation with a commercial pilot. The program culminates with a graduation flight.

ABOUT THE RESULTS:

Ninety-five percent of those enrolled in the program complete it, including the graduation flight. Although there has been no follow-up study, Dr. Scott reports that virtually all participants have reported significant improvement, and anecdotal data suggest that more than half fly regularly following the course.

Freedom to Fly groups have also received favorable press in the St. Louis area.

OHIO

PROGRAM:
Take OFF (Overcoming Fearful Flying)

WHERE:
Wright State University and Dayton General International Airport in Dayton, Ohio.

WHEN:
The program is offered two to three times a year. It consists of ten sessions over six weeks. At the time of this printing, a two-weekend program was also being developed.

SPONSORSHIP AND INSTRUCTION:
The program is cotaught by psychologist Martin Moss, Ph.D., and James Webb, Ph.D., psychologist and pilot.

COST:
$400 plus a $75 assessment fee. The optional graduation flight to Cincinnati is an additional $35.

REGISTRATION:
Write to:
>Dr. Martin Moss
>Psychology Department
>Wright State University
>Dayton, OH 45435

ABOUT THE PROGRAM:
Take OFF was begun in 1990. It is structured into group sessions that teach cognitive/behavioral coping skills. These include:

- information about flying
  (featuring guest speakers)
- relaxation training
- rethinking your fear
- graduated exposure to flying-related situations
- flight simulation
- graduation flight

ABOUT THE RESULTS:

An initial study, presented at the 1991 Aerospace Medical Association Convention, reported a 100 percent success rate for those completing the program.

WISCONSIN

PROGRAM:
Overcoming Your Fear of Flying

WHERE:
General Mitchell International Airport, Milwaukee, Wisconsin.

WHEN:
Twice a year, in February and October. The program runs four consecutive Saturdays, from 9 A.M. to noon. For additional fees, follow-up services are available throughout the year.

SPONSORSHIP AND INSTRUCTION:
Sponsored by General Mitchell International Airport; taught by Dr. Michael P. Tomaro, an aviation psychologist and certified flight instructor.

COST:
$125 for three classroom sessions and one short graduation flight.

REGISTRATION:
Class size is limited to 12, and advance reservations are required. To register, call the Community Relations Manager at (414) 747-5300, or send a check, made payable to General Mitchell International Airport, to:
General Mitchell International Airport
5300 S. Howell Ave.
Milwaukee, WI 53207
Attention: Overcoming Your Fear of Flying class

ABOUT THE PROGRAM:

The focus of Overcoming Your Fear of Flying is to provide members of the class with the skills and understanding needed to feel more comfortable about flying. To reach this goal, the class concentrates on two areas: learning about airplanes and how they fly, and learning about the causes and cures of fear. Specifically, the four classes follow this structure:

Class one: Education
- a. about critical factors associated with flight
- b. about the physiology and psychology of fear and its control

Class two: Group desensitization sessions and relaxation practice

Class three: Preflight visit to an airplane

Class four: Graduation flight

ABOUT THE RESULTS:

The program reports that approximately 85 percent of the program's participants complete their graduation flight.

WEST

CALIFORNIA

PROGRAM:
Center for Anxiety and Stress Treatment

WHERE:
The program is headquartered in San Diego but will travel to other locations upon request.

WHEN:
By appointment. Treatment is one-on-one, and the length is determined by the needs of each individual. Options include a one-week intensive program or treatment conducted over a series of weekends.

SPONSORSHIP AND INSTRUCTION:
Therapy is administered by Shirley Babior, L.C.S.W., who has treated aerophobics for 17 years. Ms. Babior is also the coauthor of *Overcoming Panic Attacks: Strategies to Free Yourself from the Anxiety Trap.*

COST:
$110 per each 45-minute session. Flight time is billed at $60 per hour.

REGISTRATION:
Contact Ms. Babior at (619) 458-1066, or write to:
Shirley Babior, L.C.S.W.
Center for Anxiety and Stress Treatment
4350 Executive Drive
Suite 204
San Diego, CA 92121

ABOUT THE PROGRAM:

This program is an option for individuals who are looking for a program tailored to their needs and conducted at their pace. The goal of treatment is to eliminate any fear-producing thoughts and behaviors that contribute to preflight anxiety and instead promote a normal mood before and during flight.

Treatment begins with an individual assessment. Cognitive and behavioral treatments include exposure in imagination (visualization) and teaching coping skills. Ms. Babior also treats any associated problems, such as panic in other situations, and teaches general stress management. Graduation flights are characterized by her individualized coaching.

ABOUT THE RESULTS:

The Center for Anxiety and Stress Treatment reports an 80 percent success rate.

PROGRAM:
Fear of Flying Clinic

WHERE:

The clinic's base of operations is at San Francisco International Airport. It utilizes several aviation facilities in the San Francisco Bay Area. It also has a branch in Australia.

WHEN:

Several times per year. Two options are available: One program is an eight-week clinic that meets Tuesday evenings for three hours, from 7 P.M. to 10 P.M. The other meets for two consecutive weekends, Saturdays and Sundays, from 9 A.M. to 5 P.M.

SPONSORSHIP AND INSTRUCTION:

The Fear of Flying Clinic is a not-for-profit public service program of the Ninety-Nines, Inc., the international organization of women pilots. It was founded and is still headed by Jeanne McElhatton and Fran Grant, both licensed pilots. The program is taught by Ninety-Nine volunteers, with active participation from the FAA, United Airlines, other major airlines, and a behavioral counselor.

COST:

$545, or $495 if you pay three weeks prior to the commencing date. Optional mini- and graduation flights are available at additional costs.

REGISTRATION:

Call (415) 341-1595 to receive a registration application, or write:

Fear of Flying Clinic
1777 Borel Place
San Mateo, CA 94402

ABOUT THE PROGRAM:

The clinic was established in 1976 and has served more than 1,000 aerophobics to date. Class sizes are limited to 25.

The program consists of lecture/discussions, field trips, and educational audiotape, films, and reading materials. Participants hear from pilots, safety instructors, air traffic controllers, flight attendants, and maintenance specialists. At the same time, a licensed behavioral counselor teaches how to change behavior through proper breathing, progressive relaxation, and cognitive reconditioning.

Clinic sessions include the study of aircraft maintenance operations; hands-on experience in plane mock-ups; a ground aircraft demonstration tour with noise experience; an air traffic control tour; and the study of airplane types and flight characteristics. A pilot lectures on "The Facts of Flight" and "Weather Phenomena."

There are two flying opportunities during the course of the clinic. A weekend "miniflight," scheduled at the clinic's halfway point, is available depending on interest and need. The optional graduation flight is round trip from San Francisco to either Los Angeles or San Diego.

ABOUT THE RESULTS:

The clinic claims a 90 percent success rate since its inception. Almost all of its clients opt to take the graduation flight, and most continue flying from then on.

PROGRAM:
Freedom to Fly

WHERE:

In Los Angeles, at the Los Angeles and Burbank airports.

WHEN:

The program is offered every other month. The groups meet six times over a four-week period.

SPONSORSHIP AND INSTRUCTION:

Administered by Ronald M. Doctor, Ph.D., a clinical psychologist with more than 20 years of experience working with panic disorders, agoraphobia, and severe phobic reactions. All instructors are psychologists with experience specific to the fear of flying.

COST:

$350.

REGISTRATION:

Contact Dr. Ron Doctor at (818) 347-0191, or write:

    Freedom to Fly
    5301 Comercio Lane
    Woodland Hills, CA 91364

ABOUT THE PROGRAM:

Freedom to Fly has been meeting in small groups since 1982. Participants are given an individualized anxiety assessment, out of which an anxiety reduction plan is formulated. They then are taught skills to control and reduce anxiety.

They also spend time learning about flying from professionals such as pilots, mechanics, and air traffic controllers. Coursework includes tours of airport facilities, operations areas, control towers, and an airplane. The final meeting is a graduation flight for those ready to take it; those who aren't can retake the course and fly later.

Freedom to Fly emphasizes an individualized approach within the group format. Group leaders are former aerophobics. The program offers follow-up services and graduate field trips, as well as continued individual consultation.

ABOUT THE RESULTS:

A two-year follow-up study found that 92 percent of participants reported improvement: They took a greater number of flights and experienced more comfort in the plane and fewer reactions to takeoff, landing, and turbulence.

PROGRAM:
TERRAP (Territorial Apprehension)

WHERE:

Locations are in San Francisco, Menlo Park, and San Jose, California. Treatment is also available through correspondence; if you live more than 200 miles away, you can take the Home Study Course.

WHEN:

The 16-week program meets once a week and is offered whenever four to seven people register. An alternative is the intensive group course, which meets all day, every day, for seven to ten days. There is also individual treatment by appointment.

SPONSORSHIP AND INSTRUCTION:

TERRAP specializes in the treatment of a wide range of phobic disorders. It was founded by Arthur B. Hardy, M.D., a past president of the Phobia Society of America (now the Anxiety Disorders Association of America), former Director of Psychiatry of El Camino Hospital, and past president of the Mental Research Institute. TERRAP's fear of flying program is taught by Edward Bourne, Ph.D., David Bezanson, Ph.D., and Cathy Pichel Cook, M.F.C.C., all specialists in the treatment of phobias and panic attack syndrome.

COST:

The 16-week group program costs $1,200 plus $100 for an individual assessment.

REGISTRATION:

Call the center at (800) 2-PHOBIA (274-6242) or (415) 327-1312.

You can also write:
TERRAP
932 Evelyn Street
Menlo Park, CA 94025

ABOUT THE PROGRAM:

TERRAP's program incorporates education, relaxation, desensitization, field work (in-vivo exposure), discussion of how thinking patterns affect behavior, communication, and assertiveness training. Specifics include visits to a flight school, lectures by a pilot, and trips to the airport and on a plane. Each person within the group progresses at her or his own pace. Participants are encouraged to bring along a support person at no extra charge.

Extra services include additional field work, either during your course or after it is finished; advanced groups and workshops for those desiring to continue treatment; and telephone help, arranged by appointment.

ABOUT THE RESULTS:

TERRAP reports that 80 percent of those who have taken the program show a "definite improvement."

PROGRAM:
THAIRAPY

WHERE:

The program is based in Newport Beach and Santa Monica, California. Seminars are held in various cities around the country.

WHEN:

Seminars are offered periodically; individual counseling is available as needed. THAIRAPY also has an audiotape flight kit that can be used at your convenience.

SPONSORSHIP AND INSTRUCTION:

THAIRAPY is directed by aviation psychologist Glen Arnold, Ph.D. Dr. Arnold has been a psychologist for more than 20 years and a pilot for 30 years. He writes a monthly column, "Aviation Psychology," for the *Pacific Flyer Aviation News.*

COST:

A four-hour seminar costs $65. The audiotape flight kits are $21.95 plus shipping. Other services: an evaluation interview costs $95; individual treatment is $95 per session; a double session is $180.

REGISTRATION:

Call (714) 756-1133, or write:
Dr. Glen Arnold, Director
THAIRAPY
4500 Campus Drive
Suite 628F
Newport Beach, CA 92660

ABOUT THE PROGRAM:

THAIRAPY was founded in 1978. It uses an integrated approach of relaxation techniques, cognitive restructuring, and desensitization to treat aerophobia. Classroom seminars range from one-half day to two-day workshops. Among the topics covered: three steps for handling turbulence; nutrition and flying; managing preflight anxiety; avoiding feelings of confinement; evaluating airline safety; five methods for controlling anxiety; and what to do the day before the flight.

THAIRAPY is also pioneering the use of aromatherapy in the treatment of aerophobia. Operating on the findings of research that show a link between scents and mood, the program has developed "flight fragrance" oils. Six fragrances are available, one to address each of the following conditions: preflight anxiety, confinement/claustrophobia, feelings of panic, labored breathing, flight-related insomnia, and the desire to increase relaxation.

The audiotape flight kit includes a flight relaxation tape, an air travel book, a wrist band, and a visualization button, together with instructions for use.

ABOUT THE RESULTS:

The program reports results better than 90 percent. It has also been featured in various publications, including the *Washington Post* and the *Los Angeles Times.*

COLORADO

PROGRAM:
Flight Without Fear

WHERE:

In Denver, Colorado, at the United Airlines Training Center.

WHEN:

The eight-week program is offered twice a year, in the fall and spring.

SPONSORSHIP AND INSTRUCTION:

Flight Without Fear is organized by the Colorado Ninety-Nines, a not-for-profit international organization of women pilots. It's offered in conjunction with United Airlines and is taught by Martha Aguilar, a licensed clinical psychologist.

COST:

Approximately $375, depending on the cost of the graduation flight.

REGISTRATION:

Contact the Colorado Ninety-Nines at (303) 278-4435 or 444-0845.

ABOUT THE PROGRAM:

Flight Without Fear is run by a staff of volunteers. They include program administrators, United Airline pilots and flight attendants, a licensed clinical psychologist, and private pilots who accompany students on the graduation flight.

The program falls into three areas of concentration:

1. Relaxation—to block the body's reaction to fear.

2. Systematic desensitization—approaching the feared situation in systematic steps designed to eliminate fear.

3. Education—programs on aerodynamics, weather, and safety. This includes tours of the United Airlines training facility, the air traffic control tower, and a parked aircraft.

ABOUT THE RESULTS:

The reported success rate is 96 percent for those who complete the program and flight.

HAWAII

PROGRAM:

The Queen's Medical Center Mental Health Clinic "Fear of Flying" program

WHERE:

The Queen's Medical Center in Honolulu, Hawaii.

WHEN:

Groups are scheduled whenever eight to ten individuals have registered. Each group consists of eight one-and-a-half-hour sessions plus a graduation flight.

SPONSORSHIP AND INSTRUCTION:

Taught by Bill Watts, M.S.W., clinical social worker specializing in anxiety-related disorders. Offered in cooperation with Hawaiian Airlines and Pacific Anxiety Resources.

COST:

Before participating in the group sessions, individuals must complete a free screening interview, a $180 intake interview, and psychological testing for $120. Each of the eight sessions is $56. The fare for the graduation flight is an additional $80.

REGISTRATION:

Call (808) 547-4401 to set up a screening interview, or write:

The Queen's Medical Center
"Fear of Flying" program
1301 Punchbowl Street
Honolulu, HI 96813

ABOUT THE PROGRAM:

The Fear of Flying program relies on an integrated approach involving education and information, in-vivo exposure, relaxation training, and cognitive restructuring. Participants share their experiences, learn the facts of flying from airline flight professionals and recovering aerophobics, and learn fear-reducing techniques. Each session builds on previous sessions, and the course culminates in a graduation flight to a neighbor island with group leaders.

ABOUT THE RESULTS:

The program reports a 90 percent success rate.

4

ADDITIONAL RESOURCES

"The computer suggests that you stay
home and clean out the attic."

4

Additional Resources

Remember that a little bit of knowledge can be dangerous, but a lot of information can be positively liberating! Finding information about airports, airlines, air traffic control procedures, travel support services, and travel destinations may help you control or even eliminate your flying fears.

If you are looking for this kind of information to help you deal with your fear of flying, there are several steps you can take.

1. Call the airport. Most large commercial airports have public relations representatives who can answer questions you might have about flying in and out of that airport. They can tell you if they or any of the airlines that use the airport offer seminars or workshops to help you overcome your fear of flying. Or they may offer to take you on a tour of the facility to familiarize you with passenger procedures, plane maintenance and preparation, preflight procedures, control tower operations, and what all those ground support personnel are really doing when you see them scrambling around the plane.

2. Contact a travel agent. Travel agents are trained to help you make the most of your travel time and dollars. As with any profession, certification identifies the most educated travel agents. A CTC (Certified Travel Counselor) designation identifies those agents with at least five years of experience who have also passed a comprehensive training program.

Many agents deal with anxious flyers on a regular basis and are more than happy to answer questions about flying, airlines, flight procedures, etc. Travel agents can also help you schedule flights at less crowded times, identify airlines that are especially customer-friendly, and help select destinations that require a minimum of connecting flights or actual flying time. And, of course, a travel agent can help you plan alternative methods of traveling and help you select a destination.

• To find a qualified travel agent, call the Institute of Certified Travel Agents at (800) 542-4282. ICTA provides a list of CTC agents in your area. You can obtain the brochure "Choosing a Great Travel Agent Is as Easy as CTC" by sending a self-addressed stamped envelope (52¢) to:

> Institute of Certified Travel Agents
> 148 Linden Street
> Wellesley, MA 02181

3. Contact a travel industry organization. Numerous travel organizations serve the traveling public, either directly or indirectly. Some provide travel information directly to the traveler, such as AAA (American Automobile Association). Others provide travel information indirectly through support services for their membership, such as ASTA (American Society of Travel Agents), which provides information to its membership on destinations, mode of travel, and travel agent/client relationships.

The travel organizations listed here provide several kinds of information:
- alternative methods of traveling
- how to choose a group tour operator
- what kinds of services a travel agency or agent provides
- travel destination details
- tips on traveling more comfortably and safely
- travel trends, issues, and statistics

• ATA - Air Transport Association of America. This organization handles research and compiles statistics about the airline industry. The association publishes the "Annual Report of the U.S. Scheduled Airline Industry" (which includes safety statistics) for $11, with a new edition released every July. It also publishes other reports and brochures. For a free catalog listing all information available, including cost, call (800) 497-3326, or write:

> Air Transport Association of America
> 1301 Pennsylvania Ave., N.W.
> Washington, D.C. 20004-1707

• AAA - American Automobile Association. This is the oldest and largest national travel and service organization for travel consumers. Members and nonmembers alike may purchase any kind of travel (air, rail, cruise, motorcoach) through AAA's extensive network of regional clubs. However, the famous AAA Triptiks, Tourbooks, and road maps that define auto travel are available only to AAA members. AAA also provides a wealth of information on travel destinations, travel safety, trends, and tips. Call the nearest AAA office listed in your phone book.

• ABA - American Bus Association. A membership organization for bus operators, the ABA offers a Motorcoach Travel Directory to consumers that lists members and types of service (charters, scheduled tours) by state and province. Call (800) 283-2877 or write:

> American Bus Association
> 1015 Fifteenth Street N.W., Suite 250
> Washington, D.C. 20005

• ASTA - American Society of Travel Agents. A professional membership organization for travel agents, ASTA provides brochures and information on how to select and use a travel agent, traveling safely, and cruise safety, among others. Its "Avoiding Travel Problems" brochure is free and available by calling (703) 739-2782 or writing to:

> ASTA Fulfillment Department
> 1101 King Street
> Alexandria, VA 22314

Enclose a self-addressed, stamped envelope for written correspondence.

• AMTRAK - The national passenger train service, Amtrak provides information to consumers through regional ticketing offices, or by calling (800) USA-RAIL

(872-7245), which provides information and reservation services.

• FAA - The Federal Aviation Administration is a federal regulatory organization for the airline industry. FAA maintains a consumer hotline that handles complaints only: (800) 835-5322.

• NTA - National Tour Association, Inc. NTA provides information primarily on motorcoach and intermodal trips. Its "Travel Together" brochures, including a listing of its members, can be obtained by calling (606) 253-1036 or writing:

> National Tour Association
> P.O. Box 3071
> Lexington, KY 40596-3071

• USTOA - The United States Tour Operators Association. A trade association for qualified tour operators, USTOA provides a free information packet to travelers, including a listing of all USTOA operators and how to select a package tour. Call (212) 944-5727, or write:

> United States Tour Operators Association
> 211 E. 51st Street, Suite 12B
> New York, NY 10022

4. Contact a State Board of Travel for destination information. Every state has a board, department, or division devoted to the promotion of travel in that state. As you will see on the following list, most have 800 numbers that allow you to call and request free travel information about destinations in that state. In addition, many large cities have Travel and Visitors Bureaus which similarly provide free information.

If flying to another state is not an option for you, you may be amazed at what interesting travel destinations are available to you within your own state or neighboring states and are accessible easily by driving, by motorcoach, or by rail. Domestic travel in the United States has grown explosively in the last ten years, and the fearful flyer has never had more nearby travel options from which to choose.

Alabama Bureau of Tourism
401 Adams Ave.
P.O. Box 4309
Montgomery, AL 36103
(800) ALABAMA

Alaska Division of Tourism
P.O. Box 110801
Juneau, AK 99811-0801
(907) 465-2010

Arizona Office of Tourism
1100 W. Washington Street
Phoenix, AZ 85007
(800) 842-8257

Arkansas Department of
    Parks & Tourism
One Capital Mall
Little Rock, AR 72201
(800) 643-8383

California Office of Tourism
801 K. Street, Suite 1600
Sacramento, CA 95814
(800) TO-CALIF

Colorado Tourism Board
1625 Broadway, Suite 1700
Denver, CO 80202
(800) 433-2656

Connecticut Tourist Division
865 Brook Street
Rocky Hill, CT 06067-3405
(800) CT-BOUND

Delaware Tourism Office
99 Kings Highway
P.O. Box 1401
Dover, DE 19903
(800) 441-8846

Florida Division of Tourism
126 W. Van Buren
Tallahassee, FL 32399-2000
(904) 487-1462

Georgia Tourist Division
P.O. Box 1776
Atlanta, GA 30301
(800) VISIT-GA

Hawaii Visitors Bureau
2270 Kalakaua Ave.
Honolulu, HI 96815
808-923-1811

Idaho Division of Travel
700 W. State Street
Boise, ID 83720
(800) 635-7820

Illinois Travel Regions:
    Chicago (800) 487-2446
    Northern Illinois
    (800) 248-6482
    Central Illinois
    (800) 262-2482
    Southern Illinois
    (800) 342-3100

Indiana Tourism Division
One North Capitol
Suite 700
Indiana, IN 46204
(800) 289-6646

Iowa Division of Tourism
200 E. Grand Ave.
Des Moines, IA 50309
(800) 345-IOWA

Kansas Travel & Tourism
  Division
700 S.W. Harrison
Suite 1300
Topeka, KS 66603-3712
(800) 2KANSAS

Kentucky Department of
  Travel Development
Capitol Plaza Tower
500 Mero Street, 22nd Floor
Frankfort, KY 40601
(800) 225-TRIP

Louisiana Office of Tourism
P.O. Box 94291
Baton Rouge, LA 70804
(800) 33-GUMBO

Maine Publicity Bureau
209 Maine Ave.
Farmingdale, ME 04344
(800) 533-9595

Maryland Office of Tourism
  Development
217 E. Redwood Street
9th Floor
Baltimore, MD 21202
(800) 543-1036

Massachusetts Office of
  Tourism
100 Cambridge Street
13th Floor
Boston, MA 02202
(800) 447-6277

Michigan Travel Bureau
P.O. Box 30226
Lansing, MI 48909
(800) 543-2937

Minnesota Office of Tourism
375 Jackson Street,
250 Skyway Level
St. Paul, MN 55101
(800) 657-3700

Mississippi Division of
  Tourism Development
P.O. Box 22825
Jackson, MS 39205-2825
(800) 647-2290

Missouri Division of Tourism
P.O. Box 1055
Jefferson City, MO 65102
(800) 877-1234

Travel Montana
Department of Commerce
1424 9th Ave.
Helena, MT 59620-0411
(800) 541-1447

Nebraska Travel & Tourism
Division
P.O. Box 94666
301 Centennial Mall South
Lincoln, NE 68509-4666
(800) 228-4507

Nevada Tourism
Commission
Capitol Complex
5151 S. Carson Street
Carson City, NV 89710
(800) 237-0774 or
(800)NEVADA8

New Hampshire Department
of Tourism
172 Pembroke Road
P.O. Box 856
(603) 271-2665

New Jersey Travel & Tourism
20 W. State Street, CN 826
Trenton, NJ 08625-0826
(800) JERSEY-7

New Mexico Department of
Tourism
491 Old Santa Fe Trail
Santa Fe, NM 87503
(800) 545-2040

New York Division of
Tourism
One Commerce Plaza
Albany, NY 12245
(800) CALL-NYS

North Carolina Travel and
Tourism
430 N. Salisbury Street
Raleigh, NC 27603
(800) VISIT-NC

North Dakota Tourism
Promotion
Liberty Memorial Building
604 East Blvd.
Bismarck, ND 58505
(800) 437-2077

Ohio Division of Travel &
Tourism
P.O. Box 1001
Columbus, OH 43266-0001
(800) BUCKEYE

Oklahoma Tourism &
Recreation
500 Will Rogers Building
Oklahoma City, OK 73105
(800) 652-6552

Oregon Tourism Division
775 Summer Street, N.E.
Salem, OR 97310
(800) 547-7842

Pennsylvania Bureau of
 Travel Development
Room 453 Forum Building
Harrisburg, PA 17120
(800) VISIT-PA

Rhode Island Tourism &
 Promotional Division
7 Jackson Walkway
Providence, RI 02903
(800) 556-2484

South Carolina Division of
 Tourism
1205 Pendleton Street
No. 106
Edgar A. Brown Building
Columbia, SC 29201
(803) 734-0122

South Dakota Department of
 Tourism
711 E. Wells Ave.
Pierre, SD 57501
(800) 843-1930

Tennessee Tourist
 Department
P.O. Box 23170
Nashville, TN 37202
(615) 741-2158

Texas Division of Travel &
 Information
P.O. Box 5000
Austin, TX 78763-5000
(800) 888-8TEX

Utah Travel Council
Council Hall - Capitol Hill
Salt Lake City, UT 84114
(801) 538-1030

Vermont Department of
 Travel & Tourism
134 State Street
Montpelier, VT 05602
(802) 828-3236

Virginia Division of Tourism
202 N. 9th Street or
1021 E. Cary Street
Richmond, VA 23219
(800) VISIT-VA

Washington, D.C. Tourism &
 Development Division
1455 Pennsylvania Ave., N.W.
Washington, D.C. 20004
(202) 789-7039

Washington Tourism
 Development Division
101 General Administration
 Building
Building AX-13
Olympia, WA 98504-0613
(800) 544-1800

West Virginia Department of
 Tourism
2101 Washington Street, East
Charleston, WV 25305
(800) 225-5982

Wisconsin Division of Tourism
P.O. Box 7970
123 W. Washington
Madison, WI 53707
(800) 432-TRIP

Wyoming Division of Tourism
Frank Norris Jr. Travel Center
I-25 & College Drive
Cheyenne, WY 82002-0240
(800) CALL-WYO

5

ALTERNATIVES TO FLYING

"...on day three you both have kitchen
duty and on day four you clean cabins!"

5

Alternatives To Flying

If, despite all your best efforts, you simply can't bring yourself to board a plane, you still have opportunities for fulfilling travel experiences. Keep in mind, however, that travel plans which don't include flying almost certainly will increase your travel time. It's especially important that you find a good, reliable travel professional who can lead you through the maze of alternative travel products with understanding and sympathy.

Your alternatives to flying are numerous. You can cruise the globe, hike in the Rockies, or travel by rail across Canada. This section will outline for you various modes of transportation, and we've provided you with contacts, addresses, and phone numbers whenever possible. This is by no means a complete list — there is a wealth of companies that cater to travelers of all kinds — but it will serve as a sampling of alternatives to get you started. For further guidance, you can contact travel associations in addition to engaging a professional travel agent. (See Section 4 for more details.)

You'll notice that we haven't included listings for Europe or other places abroad. You can adapt many of the same ideas or travel modes once you hit foreign soil, but since trans-Atlantic ship service is limited, we've restricted this information to a predominantly North American market. Once again, a travel professional can help you plan an extensive trip abroad without flying.

With the proliferation of travel services available, you can literally travel anywhere. The only limitation is your imagination.

Car Travel

Obviously, you can use your own vehicle for personal travel. If, however, you don't want to or can't use your own car, rental is an option. Car rental has become very popular with the increase in car prices over the past decade. Many travelers rent automobiles to save wear and tear on their own vehicles. Renting larger cars and minivans has also increased in popularity, as drivers have continued to "downsize" their own cars. Many residents of major metropolitan cities do not own cars, so they too find car rental a viable option for their vacation plans.

Car rental prices vary from city to city and from state to state. Airport locations are normally less expensive than city or suburban branches, so depending on where you are, it may be beneficial to pick up the vehicle near an airport.

The size of the rental car usually determines the rate. Cars may be rented on a daily, weekly, weekend, or monthly basis. Rates may be based on unlimited mileage or a per-mile fee, and drop-off charges may apply. It's very important to check drop-off fees between cities. When a car is licensed in one state, it must somehow be returned to the licensing location. This cost is passed on to the renter in the form of the drop-off fee. Don't ever assume that because states are neighbors, you can drive a rental vehicle inexpensively from one to the other and leave it there without added costs.

In addition, you must be persistent and check with a number of companies. Prices vary from company to company. Be sure to stay as flexible as possible with dates, and ask about specials or promotions pertaining to car size. Sometimes you can rent a luxury or full-sized car for the same rate as an intermediate car, given a special promotion the car rental company may be offering. If you belong to professional or travel associations or are a senior citizen, discounts may be applicable. It never hurts to ask. But, beware that many times discounts are not valid on promotional rates, so be sure to "shop."

Most car rental companies require a major credit card in the renter's name. Rates do not include gas, tax, or insurance, which are payable locally. The majority of car rental companies have minimum and maximum age requirements. To avoid adding unnecessary insurance costs to the rental, be sure to check with your own car insurance company in advance to determine if you are covered in a rental vehicle. Many car companies also charge for additional drivers.

The following are the major vehicle rental companies. You may also want to check locally, as sometimes car dealers and other local companies will rent cars.

Advantage	(800) 777-5500
Airways	(800) 952-9000
Alamo	(800) 327-9633
American International	(800) 527-0202
Avis	(800) 331-1212
Budget	(800) 527-0700
Dollar	(800) 800-4000
Enterprise	(800) 654-3131

General	(800) 327-7607
Hertz	(800) 654-3131
National	(800) 328-4300
Payless	(800) 729-5377
Snappy	(800) 669-4802
Superior	(800) 237-8106
Thrifty	(800) 331-9111
Tropical	(800) 367-5140
USA	(800) 872-2277
Value	(800) 327-2501

Recreational Vehicles

There are basically two types of recreational vehicles: towable campers and motorized vehicles. For vacation travel, the motorized vehicle (typically called the "motor home") is probably more desirable — it's the one that conjures images of the "home-away-from-home" on wheels. Most motor homes have a kitchen, bathroom, dining area, and sleeping room, all within the confines of a small traveling motorcoach area. Because a motor home is used as both transportation and accommodation, you can save a considerable amount of money on food and hotel costs. The major expense is gas, as larger motor homes average from 6 to 14 miles per gallon. Traveling by motor home is definitely for the person who enjoys driving, and it takes considerable planning to ensure a safe and enjoyable trip.

There are now more than 200 dealers who rent RVs. The rental rates vary depending on the size of the vehicle, the amenities it offers, and the length of rental. It's important to remember that motor home rental also entails additional charges such as "hook-up" in campgrounds, sewage disposal, and other fees attributed to operating the vehicle. In addition, if you rent a large motor home, you may need to rent a second vehicle for areas where the larger vehicle will be too cumbersome to maneuver.

Rather than list all the companies that rent RVs, we have listed two associations to contact. Both of these associations can give you additional information regarding the operations and rental of such equipment.

> RVIA (Recreational Vehicle Industry Association)
> P. O. Box 2999
> Reston, VA 22090
> (800) 336-0154
>
> RVRA (Recreational Vehicle Rental Association)
> 3930 University Drive
> Fairfax, VA 22030
> (800) 336-0355

RVRA publishes two booklets you may find helpful: a directory of RV rental agents that lists more than 200 dealers from across the country and Canada, and a booklet with general information and tips for having an enjoyable RV experience. The booklets are sold together for $7.50.

Bus Travel

Traveling by bus is one of the least expensive modes of transportation available. It may not be the most comfortable, the most glamorous, or the fastest way to travel, but it can be a way to get to those "out of the way" places served by no other means of transportation. Greyhound Lines is the major line, due to the fact it acquired the routes of Trailways several years ago. Greyhound has more than 2,000 buses and serves more than 200,000 cities. Usually bus passengers are allowed to stop en route, as long as their entire trip is completed by the expiration date on their ticket. Bus tickets normally are good for 60 days, but be sure to check when making your plans. Most travel agents cannot handle bus tickets, as they are not agents for the bus lines.

Keep in mind that most buses are not capable of offering food to passengers. They make frequent meal stops on long journeys, but it's advisable to pack some food. On the long-distance routes, virtually all buses have air-conditioning, toilets, and reading lamps; the short-distance routes may not. If those amenities are important to you, be sure to check them out before purchasing your ticket.

Greyhound operates in most cities; consult your local phone book for the number. There are also regional bus transportation companies that serve markets Greyhound does not, so it's best to check locally for information. Tickets for Greyhound are normally purchased at the bus station or from the driver. Independent companies have their own policies and procedures.

Motorcoach Tours / Escorted and Independent Packages

There are numerous tour operators throughout North America who plan itineraries and package their tours to be sold to the traveling public. Most of the tours operate with motorcoaches (that is, a deluxe bus). These packages are attractive because they normally include accommodations, sightseeing, transportation, and other features. Many tour operators even include meals.

Most of the companies limit participation to a set number of seats, normally governed by the size of the motorcoach. As these packages cover all parts of the United States and Canada, as well as some points in Mexico, they can be a great vacation option. All you need to do is get to the city of tour departure, wherever that might be. From that point, all arrangements are handled by the tour operator. Some operators include the services of a tour manager or escort, who handles all the arrangements en route and smooths difficulties along the way. In addition, there are some operators who plan independent itineraries with accommodations and a rental car reserved for the entire time. Other operators may specialize in city packages with accommodations, taxes, and sightseeing included.

The following list is just a beginning; with the multitude of tour operators, it would be impossible to list all of them. Since many of these companies do not take direct bookings from the public, you can consult with a professional travel agent to determine which operator has the itinerary to fit your needs.

American Express	(800) 241-1700
Brendan Tours	(800) 421-8446
California Parlor Car	(800) 227-4250
Caravan	(800) 621-8338
Cartan	(800) 422-7826
Collette	(800) 832-4656
Cosmos	(800) 221-0090
Fabulous Tours of Atlantic City	(800) 828-3344
Funway / Funjet	(800) 558-3050
Globus Gateway	(800) 221-0090
Gray Line	Varies from city to city
MTI Vacations	(800) 535-6808
Maupintour	(800) 255-4266
Princess Tours	(800) 255-4266
Sanborn Tours	(800) 395-8482
Super Cities	(800) 633-3000
Tauck Tours	(800) 468-2825
Walt Disney Travel, Inc.	(800) 327-2996 (Florida resorts) *or* (800) 824-1146 (California resorts)
Westours	(800) 426-0327

Ship and Boat Travel

Cruising has become "the" travel mode of the '90s. By getting to the point of departure, you can travel to myriad destinations without ever having to take a flight. Once you are on board, the ship becomes both hotel and transportation. Depending on your desires, you can see a variety of destinations in a somewhat limited and organized amount of time, or you can cruise for months on end.

For clarity's sake, we've listed the various cruise destination areas, with options under each category. In most instances, we've provided only long-distance numbers, as toll-free numbers may differ throughout the country. Only those lines departing from East or West Coast cities have been listed, as other points of departure would require flights (e.g., departing from San Juan and cruising to Los Angeles).

You'll notice that prices have not been listed. With the proliferation of ships in the cruise market, there are cruises for just about any budget. As a general rule, the longer the cruise — the more expensive. Accommodations on board also determine price. For instance, outside cabins are generally more expensive than inside. Certain cruise lines demand premium prices for their exceptional service, cuisine, and amenities. It's very important to research itinerary and cruise lines, so you can find your perfect "match."

Caribbean and Bahamas

A number of cruise lines sail to the Bahamas and the Caribbean. The majority of these ships sail from

Miami and Ft. Lauderdale, as well as Port Canaveral, Florida. The cruises range in length from three to ten nights. Itineraries are as varied as the lines that operate them. Getting to the Florida departure city is relatively easy from most points in the eastern United States. If you live on or near the West Coast, however, it would be less time-consuming to choose a vacation that departs from a West Coast city.

Three-night cruises generally visit Nassau and/or Freeport in the Bahamas. These short jaunts are a great way to test the waters to see if cruising is a viable and enjoyable alternative to other vacation options. Most cruise lines offer air/sea programs, so by not using the air service, you can save a considerable amount toward other cruise vacation expenses. All cruise prices include shipboard accommodations, meals, entertainment, and use of facilities. Shore excursions, gratuities, and personal items are not included.

The following is a listing of major cruise lines that operate out of Florida to destinations in the Bahamas and Caribbean.

Carnival Cruise Lines
3655 N.W. 87th Ave.
Miami, FL 33178
(305) 599-2200

Commodore Cruise Line
800 Douglas Road
Coral Gables, FL 33134
(305) 529-3000

Celebrity Cruises
5200 Blue Lagoon Drive
Miami, FL 33126
(305) 262-8322

Costa Cruise Lines
80 S.W. Eighth Street
Miami, FL 33130
(305) 358-7325

Crown Cruise Line
800 Douglas Road
Coral Gables, FL 33134
(305) 444-4600

Crystal Cruises
2121 Avenue of the Stars
Los Angeles, CA 90067
(310) 785-9300

Cunard
555 Fifth Ave.
New York, NY 10017
(212) 880-7500

Dolphin Cruise Line
901 South America Way
Miami, FL 33132
(305) 358-2111

Holland America Line
300 Elliott Ave. West
Seattle, WA 98119
(206) 281-1970

Majesty Cruise Lines
901 South America Way
Miami, FL 33132
(305) 536-0000

Norwegian Cruise Line
95 Merrick Way
Coral Gables, FL 33134
(305) 445-0886

Premier Cruise Lines
400 Challenger Road
Cape Canaveral, FL 32920
(407) 783-5061

Princess Cruises
10100 Santa Monica Blvd.
Los Angeles, CA 90067
(310) 553-1770

Regency Cruises
260 Madison Ave.
New York, NY 10016
(212) 972-4499

Royal Caribbean Cruise Line
1050 Caribbean Way
Miami, FL 33132
(305) 379-4731

Royal Cruise Line
1 Maritime Plaza
Suite 1400
San Francisco, CA 94111
(415) 788-0610

Royal Viking Line
95 Merrick Way
Coral Gables, FL 33134
(305) 447-9660

Bermuda

Ah, civilization! Bermuda is probably one destination you'll be tempted to visit time and time again. It's noted for its repeat visitor ratio — and you can travel there without flying.

Cruises to Bermuda require getting to the Big Apple, since the majority of them depart from New York City. It's relatively easy for those passengers from the East Coast, eastern seaboard, and Midwest to travel to New York. You can even combine a few days in the city prior to the cruise. The bulk of Bermuda cruises are seven days long and operate from May through October. As Bermuda is located in the Atlantic, off the coast of the Carolinas, its most popular season is during the summer months.

Listings for cruise lines that operate Bermuda cruises are as follows:

Celebrity Cruises
5200 Blue Lagoon Drive
Miami, FL 33126
(305) 262-8322

Norwegian Cruise Line
95 Merrick Way
Coral Gables, FL 33134
(305) 445-0886

Cunard
555 Fifth Ave.
New York, NY 10017
(212) 880-7500

Royal Caribbean Cruise Line
1050 Caribbean Way
Miami, FL 33132
(305) 379-4731

U.S. and Canadian Atlantic Coast

A limited number of cruise ships operate on the Atlantic Coast. Some are smaller lines that depart from

Charleston, South Carolina; Jacksonville, Florida; or points in New England. Their somewhat limited itineraries call for visits to Atlantic seaports. This option can be a great way to see coastal American cities, as well as travel between New England ports to Canadian cities via the St. Lawrence River. Most of the coastal cities are relatively easy to get to by car, rail, or bus, and this limited market provides a unique way to travel to areas not normally seen from a ship.

The following cruise lines operate cruises in this market:

American Canadian
   Caribbean Line
P. O. Box 368
Warren, RI 02885
(401) 247-0955

Crown Cruise Line
800 Douglas Road
Suite 700
Coral Gables, FL 33134
(305) 444-4600

Clipper Cruise Line
7711 Bonhomme Ave.
St. Louis, MO 63105
(314) 727-2929

Regency Cruises
260 Madison Ave.
New York, NY 10016
(212) 972-4499

Trans-Canal

Traveling through the Panama Canal has become a popular alternative to other cruise areas, especially for those looking for something a little different. Most trans-canal cruises depart from an East Coast city and end on the West Coast, or vice versa. While this makes it a little difficult without air travel, it can be done. Keep in mind a majority of these cruises begin in Los Angeles and end in Ft. Lauderdale. They are usually at least 14 days long — rarely shorter. Remember that you'll need to plan additional travel time. Depending on where you live, it may take you several days to get to the point of departure, and several more at the end of the trip to get back home. If you have ample leisure time, however, one of these cruises could be a great option.

The following are those who sail this market:

Cunard
555 Fifth Ave.
New York, NY 10017
(212) 880-7500

Royal Caribbean Cruise Line
1050 Caribbean Way
Miami, FL 33132
(305) 379-4731

Holland America Line
300 Elliott Ave. West
Seattle, WA 98119
(206) 281-1970

Royal Viking Line
96 Merrick Way
Coral Gables, FL 33134
(305) 447-9660

Princess Cruises
10100 Santa Monica Blvd.
Los Angeles, CA 90067
(310) 553-1770

Alaska/British Columbia

Alaska is a huge area — five times the size of Texas. While it's difficult to see all of Alaska without flying, you can cruise the inside passage and visit interesting ports that don't require air transportation. Alaska's tourism season is very short; it begins in mid-May and ends in mid-September, due to the weather conditions of the region. The preponderance of Alaska cruises begin in Vancouver, British Columbia, and last for seven days.

You can drive or take a train to Vancouver, or you can travel to Seattle and then take a motorcoach the rest of the way.

The listing of cruise lines follows. Some use smaller vessels, and the itineraries do vary. Be sure to check with each for further information.

Alaska Sightseeing/
   Cruise West
700 Fourth and Battery Bldg.
Seattle, WA 98121
(206) 441-8687

Costa Cruise Lines
80 S.W. Eighth Street
Miami, FL 33130
(305) 358-7325

Holland America Line
300 Elliott Ave. West
Seattle, WA 98119
(206) 281-1970

Princess Cruises
10100 Santa Monica Blvd.
Los Angeles, CA 90067
(210) 553-1770

Regency Cruises
260 Madison Ave.
New York, NY 10016
(212) 972-4499

Royal Caribbean Cruise Line
1050 Caribbean Way
Miami, FL 33132
(305) 447-9660

Trans-Atlantic Cruises

Although traveling to Europe normally requires air travel, there are certain times of the year when you can travel there via ship. A limited number of cruise lines operate sporadic trans-Atlantic crossings. Most of these crossings are "repositioning" cruises, whereby ship lines sail a vessel one way to place it in a new location to begin seasonal sailings. However, one cruise line, Cunard, offers regular service. The Queen Elizabeth II sails from New York to Southhampton, Great Britain, from May through October. With skillful planning, you can sail eastbound and then return westbound at a later date. The crossing takes five days each direction. Cunard offers a variety of accommodations and packages, as well as promotional fares. Contact them directly, or use a travel professional to assist in planning your itinerary.

Cunard
555 Fifth Ave.
New York, NY 10017
(212) 880-7500

River Cruises

The most popular cruises are aboard the Delta Queen Steamboat Company's Delta Queen and Mississippi Queen, the only two existing overnight river steamers offering service in the "Mark Twain" style. The steamboat company offers cruises down the Mississippi and Ohio rivers from various cities — New Orleans, Memphis, St. Louis, Pittsburgh, St. Paul, Cincinnati, and Chattanooga, to name just a few. These cruises offer versatility in length and scheduling, and provide a unique way to sample a slice of Americana. You can generally get to departure cities by rail, car, or bus, which makes these trips extremely attractive to Midwesterners. If you're from another part of the country, you'll find it a little more difficult, but still possible.

There are also a few companies that operate in the western states, on the Snake, Columbia, and Sacramento Rivers. Check with the companies listed below, as itineraries may vary from year to year.

Alaska Sightseeing/Cruise West
700 Fourth and Battery Building
Seattle, WA 98121
(206) 441-8687

Clipper Cruise Line
7711 Bonhomme Ave.
St. Louis, MO 63105
(314) 727-2929

Delta Queen Steamboat Company
30 Robin Street Wharf
New Orleans, LA 70130
(800) 543-1949

U. S. Pacific Coast and Mexico

There are relatively few cruise lines that sail the Pacific Coast aside from the large Mexican Riviera market. A couple of lines depart from Portland, Oregon, and cruise to Seattle, or vice versa. Or, there are some round-trip departures from San Francisco to the Napa Valley. Other cruise lines have ships in either Los Angeles or San Diego that sail weekly for seven days to the Mexican ports of Cabo San Lucas, Mazatlan, and Puerto Vallarta. This itinerary is nice, since the ships depart from large cities with easy access from most points in the West. All meals are included in the cruise fare, so it's a great way to experience Mexico without worrying about what you drink or eat. It's also a marvelous way to sail the Pacific without being away from land for very long.

Here is the listing of cruise lines that serve the Pacific Coast market:

U.S. Pacific Coast

Alaska Sightseeing/
   Cruise West
700 Fourth and Battery Bldg.
Seattle, WA 98121
(206) 441-8687

Clipper Cruise Line
7711 Bonhomme Ave.
St. Louis, MO 63105
(314) 727-2929

Mexico Market

Carnival Cruise Line
3655 N.W. 87th Ave.
Miami, FL 33178
(305) 599-2200

Princess Cruises
10100 Santa Monica Blvd.
Los Angeles, CA 90067
(310) 553-1770

Commodore Cruise Line
800 Douglas Road
Coral Gables, FL 33134
(305) 529-3000

Royal Caribbean Cruise Line
1050 Caribbean Way
Miami, FL 33132
(305) 379-4731

Norwegian Cruise Line
95 Merrick Way
Coral Gables, FL 33134
(305) 445-0886

Royal Cruise Line
1 Maritime Plaza
Suite 1400
San Francisco, CA 94111
(415) 788-0610

World Cruises

So you have a lot of time on your hands and more than a few extra dollars socked away for "that rainy day." How about a cruise around the world? It only takes 98 days, and you never have to see the inside of an airport while literally traversing the globe. World cruises normally begin in January from either Los Angeles or Ft. Lauderdale. Itineraries vary from year to year because there are repeat travelers (believe it or not!). A sample itinerary could take you from Ft. Lauderdale through the Panama Canal to the Galapagos Islands, on to the South Pacific, continuing to Indonesia and the Orient, followed by India, Egypt, Turkey, Israel, Italy, Portugal and across the Atlantic back to where the journey began. For most of us, it's the dream of a lifetime — but it could be your reality!

Companies that plan and operate world cruises:

Crystal Cruises
2121 Avenue of the Stars
Los Angeles, CA 90067
(310) 785-9300

Holland America Line
300 Elliott Ave. West
Seattle, WA 98119
(206) 281-1970

Cunard
55 Fifth Ave.
New York, NY 10017
(212) 880-7500

Train Travel

Just 50 years ago, most of the long-distance travel in the United States was still done by train. It wasn't until after World War II that the proliferation of highways and airports cut into the rail market. Today, a large section of our population has never boarded a train.

But there are those who still long to ride the rail — either for nostalgia's sake or to fulfill a first-time adventure. Train travel offers the romance of a bygone era, an unhurried experience that engages each of our senses. There is probably no more soothing sound than the clickety clack of the wheels on the tracks. The advantages to traveling by rail are many. Your only responsibility is to get to the station on time. After that, you can relax, ignore the time, and view the scenery — without worrying about stopping for gas or getting pulled over for speeding.

Rail travel also allows you to mingle with fellow passengers and make new traveling friends. In addition, train travel seems to relieve the stress of the everyday grind. You can read, eat, or just daydream as the scenery rolls by. A big part of the experience is simply enjoying getting there!

Today's trains have been modernized, and the industry is constantly working at improving amenities, service, and on-time performance. It's a relatively inexpensive mode of transportation. In some areas, such as the Northeast Corridor, train travel may be as quick as flying. With the diversity of schedules and cities served, it is possible to travel almost anywhere by train.

United States

AMTRAK (The National Railroad Passenger Corporation), was formed in 1970 by an act of Congress. The idea was to "turn around" the financially failing rail business into a stable and viable form of transportation. Since that time, AMTRAK has made a number of improvements. Trains have been upgraded, and on-time performance has improved. Personnel on board have been trained too, and food service has been overhauled. Today, AMTRAK operates more than 250 trains each day and carries more than 20 million passengers each year.

Reservations - Phone AMTRAK at (800) USA-RAIL, or contact a travel agent. Normally, there is a ticketing deadline advised at the time of booking, and tickets must be purchased by that date or the reservation will be cancelled. A reservation number is given at the time of booking as well. Be sure to note the number for future reference.

Schedules and Timetables - AMTRAK publishes timetables twice a year, which you can get at no charge by calling the toll-free number. Travel agents also usually have schedules on hand. Times shown are local times for each city. As the schedule is only printed twice a year, you should always reconfirm the desired route when you make reservations.

Fares - Fares are based on the distance traveled and the type of service or accommodations. As a general rule, rail travel is more expensive than bus but less than air. All coach is one class except for certain routes where special service is offered. The least expensive fare is the coach fare. Coach fares run from about 10¢ to 14¢ per mile for long-distance trips, but there are almost always special fares available, such as senior discounts, family fares, and excursion rates. AMTRAK's "All Aboard America Fare" has become very popular. This discount divides the country into three regions — Eastern, Central and Western. The fare is then based on the number of regions you travel through or to. These round-trip fares normally range between $200 and $300 but usually allow at least one stopover in each direction, as well as the destination point. The least expensive fare limits travel to within one region; the next higher fare to between two regions; and so on. These fares change seasonally, so be sure to check when you book.

You can pay for fares by most major credit cards, and local travel agents normally accept personal checks with local restrictions, such as required identification and sufficient time for the check to be processed. AMTRAK will also accept "prepaids," whereby one person can pay for a ticket locally, to be picked up at another city by the actual passenger. There is a nominal prepaid fee for this service, but it may be outweighed by the convenience. Most major credit cards are accepted onboard for purchases in the dining and lounge cars.

Equipment - Most of the rail fleet has been modernized and updated. Many trains have been built within the past few years. The equipment varies throughout the system but is basically as noted below:

AMFLEET — Used on short- to medium-distance routes throughout the system. Single-level coach, club, and food service cars.

HERITAGE — Used on long-distance routes in the East and midwest. Single-level coach, dining, lounge, and sleeping cars.

TURBOLINER — Used on short-distance routes in New York. Consists of single-level coach, custom class, and food service cars.

SUPERLINER — Used on routes west of Chicago. Consists of double-level sleepers, coaches, lounges, and diners.

METROLINER — Used between New York and Washington D.C. Offers reserved seating on one-level coaches.

AUTO TRAIN — Carries passengers and automobiles between Lorton, Virginia, and Florida. Offers sleepers, dome, diner, and lounge, as well as enclosed carrier cars for automobiles.

Accommodations - Provisions for seating, sleeping, food, and storage vary according to the train type. The accommodations available are as follows:

COACH SEATING — All trains have coach cars. There are two reclining seats on each side of a 23-inch-wide aisle. All have overhead reading lights. You can place luggage in overhead racks above the seats on both sides of the aisle. All cars have restrooms whose locations differ based on the type of equipment. Coach seats used for overnight long-distance travel have leg rests that fold out from under each seat. On Superliner, Turboliner, and Amfleet, cars offer fold-down trays on the back of each seat. Seat width ranges from 19 to 20 inches. Pillows are provided to all coach passengers traveling on overnight trains.

CLUB SERVICE — (offered only on Amfleet, Metroliner, and Turboliner trains) Features reserved deluxe seating with at-your-seat food and beverage service. The car has a single seat on one side of a 31-inch-wide aisle and two seats on the other side. Overhead luggage racks, individual reading lights, and fold-down trays are at each seat.

CUSTOM CLASS SEATING — Reserved seat, self-serve coffee, tea, or juice, and newspaper. Offered only on Amfleet, Metroliner, and Turboliner trains. Seats also have overhead luggage racks, individual lights, and fold-down trays.

BAGGAGE — You can check up to three pieces of luggage not exceeding 75 pounds each or total weight not to exceed 150 lbs. Baggage may be checked through to your final destination even if you make train connections. You can carry two pieces of personal luggage on board in the coach compartment, as long as they fit in the overhead compartments or special storage areas. Sleeping car passengers may stow in their compartment as many suitcases as the space can accommodate.

SLEEPING ACCOMMODATIONS — Sleeping accommodations are available at an additional charge to the coach fare. The accommodations vary from train to train. On western routes, sleeping car accommodations frequently sell out months in advance during the busy summer months, so make reservations early.

FOOD SERVICE — With the exception of short haul trains, meal service is available on most AMTRAK trains. Full meal service is available on all overnight, long-distance routes. Dining cars offer meals prepared on board, served with tablecloths and china. Meals in the dining room are complimentary with the purchase of roomettes or bedrooms on the Heritage, and with the purchase of economy, deluxe, family, or special bedrooms on the Superliner. Budget-priced slumber coach rooms do not qualify for complimentary meal service. For first-class service, coffee is served from 6:30 to 9:30 each morning. Special meal services are also offered with 72 hours' notice. Kosher, low sodium/cholesterol, and at-seat or in-room meal service (for those with limited mobility) are all available.

SMOKING — Effective May 1993, smoking is prohibited on certain trains with travel time less than four and a half hours. There is no smoking allowed in lounge cars and dining cars, but there is a designated smoking area on some trains. Be sure to ask if you are concerned.

Canada

As in the United States, Canada designated the operation of its passenger rail service to a government-owned corporation, VIA Rail Canada. Prior to 1990, there were two transcontinental routes, one going through Edmonton, the other through Calgary. But in 1990, the government cut back drastically on the service, leaving only the route through Edmonton intact. These long-distance trains now operate only three times a week. In the east, you can connect with the Canadian system on AMTRAK from New York. There are also ways to connect Chicago and Toronto. To mesh the two itineraries, use the services of a travel professional.

Reservations - Reservations are required for VIA 1, first-class, and sleeping car accommodations. Telephone (800) 361-3677 or see your local travel agent. You can make reservations up to six months in advance of departure date. Ticketing deadline is given at time of booking. Reservations are automatically canceled if not ticketed by that date.

Schedules and timetables - Published twice a year. You can obtain them by telephoning the toll-free number above.

Fares - The cost of rail travel in Canada is generally comparable to the cost of travel on AMTRAK. VIA Rail does, however, offer special discounts and senior and student discounts. It also offers a Canrailpass, which allows unlimited rail travel for one fixed price. Call for more information. You can use major credit cards to pay for fares, as well as on-board services.

Equipment - In Canada, the equipment is generally older than that in the United States. However, it has been well maintained and in many instances refurbished. The new LRC (Light Rapid Comfortable) trains have gone into service in some markets, mostly the highly populated areas among Toronto, Quebec, and Montreal.

Accommodations - VIA Rail Canada's equipment is similar to the Heritage fleet of AMTRAK. There are sections, roomettes, and bedrooms offered on the transcontinental service and VIA 1, which is first-class service similar to club service on AMTRAK. Be sure to check the route and train for accommodations offered.

Baggage - Up to 100 pounds of luggage may be checked per adult. As with AMTRAK, you can bring personal luggage on board.

Food service - Similar to AMTRAK.

Smoking - Most areas of the train are nonsmoking. Smoking is permitted in the enclosed space of sleeping cars and in designated areas of coaches and lounge cars. Pipes and cigars are prohibited.

Ecotourism

"Ecotourism" — that is, socially and environmentally responsible travel — has become a fast growth area in the '90s. This type of travel encompasses what we might call "soft adventure"; it covers a variety of activities that offer exciting and enjoyable opportunities without flying. In most cases, these travel options involve some connection with nature. Most ecotourists like outdoor activities and are willing to share experiences with others.

These trips span a wide range of physical skills; there's something for everyone, regardless of age or energy level. You can challenge your abilities, or you can enjoy the scenery lazily while someone else does the work.

Bicycling

Bicycling has been steadily increasing in popularity for the last several years. Cyclists band together for both short trips and lengthy expeditions. The equipment has become more and more sophisticated, making this mode of travel comfortable for cycling enthusiasts as well as those just looking for a "different" kind of vacation. Bicycle trails have cropped up in major cities across the country, and the "rails-to-trails" movement has converted many abandoned railroad tracks to hike/bike trails, which sometimes link cities to each other.

The cycling trend has given rise to numerous companies that operate and plan bicycle trips. Many of these tour operators provide bikes, accommodations, and detailed maps. They'll also customize vacations to the individual's needs. Most itineraries involve overnight stops at inns and hotels. A typical group may consist of eight to thirty cyclists and a support van that literally does what its title suggests: It carries the food, luggage, and any cyclists who need a rest. Details of the trip can vary, however, depending on the area, length of the trip, and interests of the cyclists. If you haven't done much cycling, you may want to try a weekend trip before tackling an extended journey.

The following is a list of some companies that can assist in planning a bicycling trip. There are also companies that specialize in smaller regions of the country. Check with your local cycling club to see if they can recommend a tour operator in your area.

> Backroads Bicycle Touring
> 1516 5th Street, Suite 1C10
> Berkeley, CA 94710
> (800) 245-3874

Tours from 2 to 16 days. Bicycling routes for all ages and abilities. In business for more than 12 years. Support van carries luggage, etc.

Brooks Country Cycling
140 W. Third Street
New York, NY 10024
(212) 874-5151
In business for more than 16 years. Year-round bicycle tours for adults and families. Extensive program of more than 200 tours, from day trips to weekends and week-long vacations. Tours designed for all levels.

Timberline Bicycle Tours
P. O. Box 18324
Boulder, CO 80308
(303) 499-8965
In its 11th season. Will stage a large selection of tour options. Tours in Colorado, California, Michigan, Minnesota, and Wisconsin, to name a few. Programs range from 5 to 9 days and cover basically the western United States and northern Great Lakes.

VCC Four Seasons Cycling
P. O. Box 145, Dept. 232
Waterbury, VT 05677
(802) 244-5135
In business 13 years. Casual bicycle tours from weekends to week-long. Destinations include Florida, Maine, Maryland, Massachusetts, New Hampshire, North Carolina, Nova Scotia, and Ottawa, to name a few.

Hiking

What better way to explore the world than by using your own two feet? Hiking has been a travel option since the dawn of humanity. Often it was the only mode of transportation available. Although we now have a bounty of modes to choose from, hiking remains a viable option for exploring the wilderness without needing great athletic ability or a lot of cumbersome equipment. Your only real necessities are a pair of well-made sneakers for easy terrain and a pair of hiking boots for the more difficult areas.

Companies that run hiking trips — "outfitters," as they're called — provide scheduled departures and will help you plan a safe, secure trip. Some of the same companies that plan bicycle tours also handle hiking trips. You may want to consider having one of them plan a "combo" trip for you, so you can spend your vacation both hiking and biking.

Country Walkers
P. O. Box 180S
Waterbury, VT 05675
(802) 244-1387
Offers 2- to 12-day educational walking tours for adults in Maine, the Sonoran Desert of Arizona and Washington's Olympic Peninsula. Four to 9 miles per day on easy to moderate terrain. In business for 14 years.

Knapsack Tours
5961 Zinn Drive
Oakland, CA 94611
(415) 339-0160

Inexpensive moderate day hikes without backpacks. Small groups, personally guided: Canadian Rockies, Olympic National Park, Yosemite, California, and others.

Glacier Wilderness Guides
P. O. Box 535A
West Glacier, MT 59936
(406) 862-4802
Glacier National Park's only backpacking guide service. One-half-day to 6-day trips. Caters to groups of all ages and sizes.

Roads Less Traveled
Box 18742
Boulder, CO 80308
(303) 530-4802
Offers hiking and biking trips from 2 to 6 days. All abilities. Rocky Mountain specialists offering Utah canyon lands, Colorado national parks and Santa Fe/Taos region.

Rafting

The Colorado and Snake rivers have become almost synonymous with rafting. Each year, countless visitors to the Grand Canyon area take rafting trips — often combined with other sightseeing options. But rafting is not limited to this area. Nearly every state has rafting outfitters that will arrange trips for anywhere from a few hours to a week or more. The outfitters provide the equipment, information, and personnel to ensure that your trip is enjoyable.

We've listed a few companies below. Also, be sure to check with local, state, and national parks. Nature clubs and other outdoor organizations may be able to give recommendations, too.

> Adrift Adventures
> P. O. Box 574
> Moab, UT 84532
> (800) 874-4483

Wide selection of trips, from 1/2 day to 8 days. Trips available on the Green and Colorado Rivers in Utah and on the Flathead and Lochsa rivers in Montana and Idaho.

> Action Whitewater Adventures
> P. O. Box 1634
> Provo, UT 84603
> (800) 453-1482

Rafting trips offered in Idaho, California, and Arizona.

> Grand Canyon Dories
> P. O. Box 216
> Altaville, CA 95221
> (209) 736-0805

Trips range from 5 to 20 days on various sections of the Colorado River. Billed as the "ultimate" Grand Canyon river trip.

> O.A.R.S. (Outdoor Adventure River Specialists)
> P. O. Box 67
> Angels Camp, CA 95222
> (800) 346-0805

In business 20 years. Specialists on the Colorado River through the Grand Canyon. Also offers trips through Grand Teton National Park, on the San Juan and Dolores Rivers in Utah and numerous others.

Unicorn Rafting Expeditions
P. O. Box Dept. 47
Brunswick, ME 04011
(207) 725-2255

Offering trips on the Kennebec and Penobscot Rivers in Maine and the Hudson and Moose Rivers in New York. Wide variety of trips to suit just about everyone.

Wildwater Expeditions Unlimited, Inc.
P.O. Box 55
Thurmond, W. VA 25936
(800) 982-7238

Offers trips on the New and Gauley Rivers in West Virginia. Most trips average 5 hours and are available for beginners as well as experienced rafters.

Covered Wagons

The idea of modern-day covered wagon trips began in conjunction with the centennial celebration in the state of Kansas. Since then, operators have developed programs so that would-be pioneers can relive the experience of their forebears.

It's hard to believe the American pioneers actually traveled across the country in these small covered wagons. The pace is only about 20 miles per day. While this experience may not be for everyone, it's something out of the ordinary, and it could be a great choice for families.

Oregon Trail Wagon Train
Rt. 2 Box 502-A
Bayard, NE 69334
(308) 586-1850

Offers 1/2-day, 24-hour, and 3- to 6-day wagon train treks along the Oregon Trail. Cookouts, canoeing, and other activities.

Wagons West
Peterson-Madsen Taylor Outfitters
Box 1156A
Afton, WY 83110
(307) 886-9693

Offers 2-, 4-, and 6-day wagon train treks in the Jackson Hole-Grand Tetons area of Wyoming.

Want To Send a Copy of
The Fearful Flyers Resource Guide
to a Friend or Family Member?

Please complete the form below,
and mail it with a check or money order to:

Argonaut Entertainment, Inc.
455 Delta Avenue, Suite 204
Cincinnati, Ohio 45226

(Please Allow Four Weeks For Delivery)

ORDER FORM

Please send me _____ copies of

The FEARFUL FLYERS Resource Guide @ $13.95 ea. = _____

plus $3.00 shipping/handling for each book.   = _____

Total Amount Enclosed   = _____

(Please make check payable to Argonaut Entertainment.)

Book(s) should be mailed to: (please print)

_____
Name

_____
Street

_____
City   State   Zip

Want To Send a Copy of
The Fearful Flyers Resource Guide
to a Friend or Family Member?

Please complete the form below,
and mail it with a check or money order to:

Argonaut Entertainment, Inc.
455 Delta Avenue, Suite 204
Cincinnati, Ohio 45226

(Please Allow Four Weeks For Delivery)

ORDER FORM

Please send me _____ copies of

The FEARFUL FLYERS Resource Guide @ $13.95 ea. = _____

plus $3.00 shipping/handling for each book.　　= _____

Total Amount Enclosed　　　　　　　　　= _____

(Please make check payable to Argonaut Entertainment.)

Book(s) should be mailed to:　(please print)

_____
Name

_____
Street

_____
City　　　　　　　　　State　　　　Zip